EMBRACING YOUR FREEDOM

A Personal Experience of God's Heart for Justice

susie larson

MOODY PUBLISHERS
CHICAGO

All Scripture quotations, unless otherwise indicated, are taken from the *Holy Bible, New Living Translation*®, nlt®. Copyright © 1996, 2004. Used by permission of Tyndale House Publishers, Inc., Wheaton, Illinois 60189, U.S.A. All rights reserved.

Scripture quotations marked msg are from *The Message*, copyright © by Eugene H. Peterson 1993, 1994, 1995. Used by permission of NavPress Publishing Group.

Scripture quotations marked amp are taken from *The Amplified Bible*. Copyright © 1965, 1987 by The Zondervan Corporation. The Amplified New Testament copyright © 1958, 1987 by The Lockman Foundation. Used with permission.

Scripture quotations marked esv are taken from *The Holy Bible, English Standard Version*. Copyright © 2000, 2001 by Crossway Bibles, a division of Good News Publishers. Used by permission. All rights reserved.

Scripture quotations marked nkjv are taken from the *New King James Version*. Copyright © 1982 by Thomas Nelson, Inc. Used by permission. All rights reserved.

Scripture quotations marked niv are taken from the *Holy Bible, New International Version*®. niv®. Copyright © 1973, 1978, 1984 by International Bible Society. Used by permission of Zondervan. All rights reserved.

Scripture quotations marked hcsb are taken from *The Holman Christian Standard Bible* © 2001, Broadman & Holman Publishers, Lifeway Christian Resources, 127 Ninth Avenue North, Nashville, Tennessee 37234. All rights reserved.

Emphasis was added to Scripture by the author.

All International Justice Mission casework stories have been used with the permission of IJM. Pseudonyms have been used to protect the clients IJM serves. Casework documentation and real names are on file at IJM's Washington, D.C., headquarters.

Published in association with the literary agency of Alive Communications, Inc., 7680 Goddard Street, Suite 200, Colorado Springs, CO 80920, www.alivecommunications.com <http://www.alivecommunications.com/>.

Editor: Jane Johnson Struck
Interior Design: David LaPlaca/debestdesignco.
Cover Design: LeVan Fisher Design
Cover Images: © Dimitri Vervitsiotis/Getty Images, Stockbyte/Getty Images, and Colin Anderson/Getty Images

Library of Congress Cataloging-in-Publication Data
Larson, Susie
    Embracing your freedom : a personal experience of God's heart for justice / Susie Larson.
        p. cm.
    Includes bibliographical references (p.   ).
    ISBN 978-0-8024-5280-1
    1. Liberty—Religious aspects—Christianity. 2. Justice—Religious aspects—
Christianity. 3. Christianity and justice. 4. Rescue work—Religious aspects—Christianity.
5. International Justice Mission. I. Title.
    BT810.3.L37 2009
    241'.675—dc22

                                                                            2009021788

We hope you enjoy this book from Moody Publishers. Our goal is to provide high-quality, thought-provoking books and products that connect truth to your real needs and challenges. For more information on other books and products written and produced from a biblical perspective, go to www.moodypublishers.com or write to:

Moody Publishers
820 N. LaSalle Boulevard
Chicago, IL 60610

1 3 5 7 9 10 8 6 4 2

Printed in the United States of America

Susie Larson's call to women to not only discover their freedom in Christ but also to embrace it rings true because it issues from a humble, guileless heart. Larson knows what it's like to be bound up in spiritual and emotional prisons—some of our own making, some by others. She also knows the release of discovering that we no longer have to stay in those prisons unless we choose to do so. *Embracing Your Freedom* is more than a practical discipleship tool—though it is certainly that—but it is also a compelling invitation to begin to move into all the joys and adventures that await us as women of the Most High God. Larson doesn't just point the way; she leads us there with her stories and examples and challenges. It's a journey you won't want to miss.

> —**Kathi Macias**, author of *Mothers of the Bible Speak to Mothers of Today*

Embracing Your Freedom was written for you—a woman who desires to live in personal freedom and is willing to help the helpless become free. Prepare to be challenged and emboldened. Prepare to change and become more like Jesus!

> —**Kendra Smiley**, conference speaker, and author of *Be the Parent, Journey of a Strong-Willed Child,* and *Do Your Kids a Favor . . . Love Your Spouse.*

Embracing Your Freedom is the book for women that's needed to be written for a long time! What Susie's gotten exactly right is the divine coherence between the God who redeems the hearts of individuals and the One who liberates those who are bound by injustice. In fact, for God—and for Susie!—these two are inextricably linked. In this important book, Susie invites women into life that really is life by naming them, naming us, as agents made to extend God's justice to those who are bound. Women today are hungry for this kind of holy congruity. Thank you, Susie!

> —**Margot Starbuck**, author of *The Girl in the Orange Dress: Searching for a Father Who Does Not Fail*

From Latin America to India, the Philippines, and Afghanistan, I've personally witnessed the despair of exploited children, abused women, widows, and orphans. Like author Susie Larson, I've wept because I can't rescue them all. International Justice Mission is a powerful instrument of God's justice in that darkness, and *Embracing Your Freedom* offers a powerful message of inner liberation along with God's heart of love for the oppressed.

—**Jeanette Windle**, author of *Veiled Freedom and Betrayed*

In *Embracing Your Freedom*, Susie Larson vividly demonstrates that the path to embracing our own freedom is aligned with advocating for the freedoms of others. Whether the bondage is to abusive traffickers or to the lies of Satan, freedom comes only through the power of Jesus Christ and His truth.

—**Vonda Skelton**, national speaker and author of *Seeing Through the Lies: Unmasking the Myths Women Believe*

To the woman who is literally free and wants to be totally free
*You are living in an important day. May God give you
a holy passion to be everything He intended you to be!*

To the slave who waits for rescue
*I pray for you every day.
May the message in this book mobilize many on your behalf!*

To my justice girlfriends Susan Ivancie and Sara Groves
*I don't have words to express my love and respect for you both.
It's been an honor serving alongside you. ·*

To International Justice Mission
*Thank you for confronting the world's bullies
and for standing up for the voiceless.
You are all my heroes.*

To Kevin
*Thank you for giving so much of yourself on behalf of those in need.
I absolutely cherish the journey we are on together.*

To Jesus
You show me every day what it means to be Yours. I love You most of all.

CONTENTS

Not their real names

Not their real names

FOREWORD

I often look over a room of women and am moved to tears at the possibilities. We are wonderfully wired for compassion and strength, and can accomplish so many things. But I also sigh heavily over our innate ability to sabotage our own freedom. I know from my own life how easily our perspective can be skewed by anxiety, relational turmoil, and attempts at control, and how easily we lose sight of the larger purpose in our daily burdens.

But God calls us to become free, and to the extent that we lay hold of this freedom, we will fulfill a greater purpose for our lives! There is nothing more beautiful than a woman who is free, and there is no more compassionate freedom fighter than a woman who is free. I have seen God leverage a woman's great compassion and strength when she finds freedom for herself and begins to seek freedom for others.

The working out of our salvation led Susie and me to a greater desire to be the hands and feet of Christ in our world. That opportunity became real for us through the work of International Justice Mission (IJM), a faith-based human rights agency that for more than a decade has worked to bring the Good News to and secure justice for victims of slavery, sexual exploitation, and other forms of violent oppression (visit www.IJM.org to learn more). This adventure has led us to chair a local IJM event in Minnesota, and most recently to visit Capitol Hill, where we advocated together for new legislation to help end the trafficking of children.

With tremendous grace and love for the reader, Susie Larson brings us stories of Good News from her own life and from the lives of those rescued from slavery. It is my prayer that as you read these pages you will be challenged and inspired to embrace the reality of God's freedom in your own life, and in response to that freedom become the miracle so many are waiting for!

—*Sara Groves*

For yet a little while and the wicked shall be no more;
Indeed, you will look carefully for his place,
But it shall be no more.
But the meek shall inherit the earth,
and shall delight themselves in the abundance of peace.
—PSALM 37:10–11 NKJV

LET'S START HERE . . .

You're blessed when you get your inside world—your mind and heart—put right. Then you can see God in the outside world.

—MATTHEW 5:8 MSG

No one who really wants to count for God can afford to play at Christianity.[1]

—H. A. IRONSIDE

Are you free? I mean *truly* free? I'm on my way there, but I still have some land to reclaim. I've been a Christian for more than thirty years, so I'm freer now than I was ten years ago. I'm truer now than I was back then. I know more now than I did last week. However, I still have places within me that have yet to be freed. But I want everything God intends for me. And I want it for you as well.

When I pray, "May Your Kingdom come and Your will be done *on earth*, as it is in heaven . . . ," I find myself increasingly hungry to experience the reality of this prayer. In heaven there's no bondage, no fear, no assault, no lack.

Ponder this verse's meaning: *In just a little while, the wicked will be no more;* though you look *carefully at his place,* he will not be there. *But the meek shall inherit the land and delight themselves in abundant peace* (Psalm 37:10–11 ESV, emphasis mine).

Imagine an area of your life occupied by defeat, fear, or manipulation. Maybe you're on the brink of divorce or have no peace with your neighbor. Maybe you're wracked with pain over a wayward child. Or maybe your sense of safety has been shattered and you distrust others.

Now imagine the Enemy is shoved off your land. The space he once possessed—where he had continual access to torment and threaten you—is recovered. Picture freedom and wholeness and abundant peace. Breathe it in.

Where once you had fear, you have faith. Where once you had anxiety, you have assurance. Where once you were suspicious, you believe the best. Where once you walked on eggshells, you walk boldly in faith. Where once thorns and thickets choked, abundant fruit grows, fruit that nourishes you and blesses *others*.

The Lord loves righteousness and justice; the earth is full of his unfailing love.

(Psalm 33:5 niv)

The thief came to steal, kill, and destroy. But Jesus came that we might have life, life abundant, life to its fullest, restored, whole, and free (see John 10:10).

This Enemy of our souls is ruthless. He beats and bruises us. He kicks us when we're down, steals what matters to us, and distorts the truth. He is ruthless on all levels and everything he does is based on a lie. He is perfectly giddy at the thought of robbing us blind.

But then there's God. We serve a God deeply motivated by love and profoundly committed to freedom. A God so mighty that even mountains melt like wax in His presence and ocean floors open at the blast of His breath. This same God loves us fiercely and calls us to participate in His divine nature. In addition to the salvation He offers us (which in itself is gift enough), He wants us *free* on earth.

God wants us to stand strong in the face of our giants, our bullies, and our scary circumstances. He longs for us to enjoy an abundance of peace. He doesn't want us to be pushed around by our fears. God knows that sometimes the Enemy gets away with his schemes, but when we take Him at His Word, He helps us get back what we've lost—and then some.

What has the Enemy stolen from *you*? Are you constantly broke, sick, or afraid? God wants you whole, healed, and assured of His protection. Was your childhood lost to a ruthless upbringing? God wants to restore everything you lost when life let you down. Does your child hate you, or has your spouse abandoned you? God will never leave you or forsake you, and He will carry you through the darkest times. Maybe a bad business decision or a corrupt business partner has left you clinging to what few earthly possessions you have, and now faith seems elusive. Even if you feel as though God is miles away, He's intimately near and fully engaged with you on this journey.

Not every loss is replaceable; we can't replace our children or our childhood. Yet God can restore what the Enemy steals. He can redeem fear and sorrow. He can make up for lost time. He's terrific at creating those sudden supernatural breakthroughs—where one moment you're imprisoned and the next you're free; where one moment your dream dies, and the next God resurrects an even better one.

God cares about you. And whatever "land" you've lost, He wants you to recover. Even the land you handed over because of unbelief or missteps. Don't give up hope. His promises are true and His heart beats for you!

However, please note that if you can afford this book, you already enjoy a measure of freedom. There are women around the world whose struggle is so deep, whose bondage is so severe, that for them freedom seems an impossibility.

God notices every man, woman, and child who suffers at the hands of evil people. His heart burns for the sex-trafficking victim violated many times a day. He weeps for the modern-day slave who toils alongside her husband and children eighteen hours a day in a rice mill. His anger burns every time someone is beaten. God thinks about these precious souls as much as He thinks about you. Indeed, the millions victimized by violent injustice today are never far from our Father's thoughts.

God cares about the marginalized and the overlooked. He notices the poor. He walks through the slums and beckons His followers to meet Him there, to be His hands and feet. We serve a mighty God. Not a Western God, not even an American God, but a God of all humanity. He's a God of justice. And one day, God's mighty fist will come down like a powerful gavel and ultimate justice will prevail. In the meantime, though, He does His Kingdom work through *you and me.*

Part of what it means to embrace freedom is to become an advocate for the freedoms of others. God calls us to love mercy, to do justice, and to walk humbly with Him (see Micah 6:8).

Gary Haugen, founder and president of International Justice Mission (IJM), knows the pain of these abuse victims well. IJM's team of lawyers, investigators, and social workers stands on the front lines to bring freedom to these precious sisters and brothers around the world. After seeing their suffering up close, Gary became convinced that we "have a God of moral clarity. God does not respond to injustice or abuse with mild interest."[2]

God wants all of us free because that's who He is. That's how He is.

It's my earnest desire that as you read this book, you become better acquainted with the One who loves your soul. With an ever-increasing understanding of what you possess in the person of Christ, may you grow tenacious in taking back the land He intended for you in the first place, because through Him, *you can.*

I also pray that as you read, you find yourself more aware of the afflictions of your sisters around the world: the woman in literal slavery and the one betrayed into human trafficking; the woman bullied off of her land and the one whose child is stolen. These women matter to us; their problems are our problems. And when we pray for them, their fruit becomes our fruit, their victory our victory.

As you become more aware of God's heart for freedom, your heart will burn for it as well. If you will dare to put your foot down on the promises of God and refuse to relent until freedom becomes *your reality*, your appetite for the freedoms of others will increase as well. Take seriously what God has offered you here, because as a Believer living in this day, you are in a powerful position of influence.

The world's spiritual climate of bondage changes every time you earnestly pray for the liberty of one in literal chains. With every fervent prayer, with every mustard seed of faith, true freedom becomes possible. *The prayer of a person living right with God is something powerful to be reckoned with* (James 5:16 MSG).

It's for freedom Christ set us free. May we refuse to be subject to slavery's yoke. May we open our eyes to others' sufferings so they may enjoy the literal freedoms we do.

Isn't it amazing to think that the God who crafted the mountains and seas cares profoundly about one woman's life as though she were the only one on earth? He sees her face. He knows her name. He knows her story—by heart. He loves her spirit. He'll leave the group to go get her. He'll move heaven and earth for her. He'll go through hell to rescue her. In fact, He already has. He wants her saved. He wants her restored. That girl is *you*.

And . . . she's also the one still awaiting rescue. God's heart is that big.

There's so much more of God to know and experience! That's

why we're here. We've got a great journey ahead. Take your time working through each chapter. Approach the *Initiate Your Freedom* questions with focus, honesty, and courage. You'll be challenged and changed as a result.

Between each section of this book you'll read a story of a young woman, one like you and yet altogether different. Hers is a journey from literal captivity to rescue, from injustice to justice. Her story will grip you, affect your thinking, and compel you to be a conduit for freedom.

I'm excited to make this journey with you. I'll be praying for you as you work your way through these pages. May the Lord Jesus Himself breathe fresh life into your soul and completely overhaul your thinking! And may He infuse you with fresh courage as you take His hand and walk away from captivity into new places of promise.

But a little caution here: this book isn't exactly light reading. It's for the woman who wants to grow stronger in her faith and gain a greater view of God's heart for the world. God calls us to gritty faith so our lives might have eternal significance. So consider the coming weeks as a boot camp that will challenge, stretch, and strengthen your soul.

May you be provoked to be as free as God meant you to be. And as a result, may you become an advocate for the freedoms of others.

May the Lord bless you as you read.

 **_Precious and intimate Father,_**

What can I say except thank You for loving me? Where would I be if not for You? Help me to let go of my fears and insecurities and open wide my soul to Your divine influence! I want to be free! I am free because of You. I'll keep declaring it until I know it full well. You are my deliverer; You are all that I need! Bless Your beautiful name. Take me by the hand and lead me to new places of freedom.

And now, Lord, I pray for those in captivity. Bless their hearts. Give them faith. Protect their souls. Set them free. Confuse and expose the plans of evil men and establish the plans of Your people. Break the bonds of modern-day slavery! Set captives free! Hear my cry; add it to the numbers who cry out day and night for their rescue! Protect those You've appointed as rescuers. Remind me to pray for their safety every day. Thank You for these modern-day heroes. In Jesus' name, I pray. Amen.

section one

FACING EVIL,
RECOVERING
WHAT'S OURS

Sandana's* Story[1]

It is for freedom that Christ has set us free. Stand firm, then, and do not let yourselves be burdened again by a yoke of slavery.
—Galatians 5:1 NIV

Whenever I hear anyone arguing for slavery, I feel a strong impulse to see it tried on him personally.[2]
—Abraham Lincoln

Young Sandana and her family, along with approximately twenty other slaves, were held captive by a brutal set of slave owners. These precious slaves toiled relentlessly for long hours every day in a South Asian rice mill. The slave owners beat the slaves, sexually violated the women, and cruelly punished one slave by dousing his arm in kerosene and lighting it on fire. Even the International Justice Mission (IJM) investigators were attacked while attempting to secure freedom for these slaves.

And yet, amidst such evil, God used Sandana*—a brave twelve-year-old slave girl—to bring down these despicable men. Because young Sandana spoke up, the slaves were released.

Not her real name. A similar version of this story first appeared in Gary Haugen's book Just Courage.

This is how the story played out: The IJM investigators helped police mobilize a raid on the rice mill and the slaves were brought before the local magistrate. There they had the chance to tell their story. But because they had been so traumatized at the rice mill, when faced with the opportunity to tell the truth, they denied their torture and enslavement. The power of the threat against them was stronger than the promise of freedom before them. Fear of retaliation compelled these captives to stay captive.

One by one the slaves denied to the magistrate that they were held against their will or abused. Despair engulfed the IJM investigators as they pictured the slaves slipping back into bondage. Their hard work would come to nothing.

Things looked truly hopeless. Then something amazing happened. Young Sandana found the courage to do what the bullies most feared: *she spoke the truth.*

To her parents' horror, Sandana stepped forward and explained that she and the other slaves were indeed enslaved and endured terrible treatment from the owners. She explained the reason her dad and the others didn't tell the truth; they were too afraid of the evil men who held them captive. Struck by the raw power of innocent truth, the magistrate said he thought a young child would not lie about such things.

> When justice is done, it brings joy to the righteous but terror to evil-doers. (PROVERBS 21:15 NIV)

Emboldened, Sandana's father and the other slaves now confirmed her story—in fact, they told of other slaves still hidden away at the rice mill.

The truth gave these slaves the courage to tell more truth, which in turn destroyed the plans of the Enemy and secured freedom for the others.

Because of Sandana's bravery, she and a whole community of former slaves now are free. The children are attending school and their families are building independent lives in which they can make choices about work and food, about life and love.

Sandana's story speaks for the millions of slaves in our world today. In fact, more slaves exist now than during the three hundred–plus years of transatlantic slave trade! Twenty-seven million people —created in God's image—are held and abused today, against their will, and they hope against hope for a chance to be free.

Approximately two-thirds of today's slaves are in South Asia. Human Rights Watch estimates that in India alone, there are as many as 15 million children in bonded slavery.[3]

Most reading this book enjoy liberties these precious slaves would find difficult to comprehend. What an exorbitant privilege to hop into the car and drive to a coffeehouse for a $4 cup of coffee. What a treasured freedom to decide whether or not to go to bed early. Taking our kids to the park, enjoying a day at the beach, devouring Christian books, praying in broad daylight, watching back-to-back movies on a cold, rainy day: all of these priceless gems make us rich indeed.

Yet some of the greatest believers who have walked this planet were freer as literal slaves than many of us who are literally free but not totally free. Our slavery might be figurative, yet it still keeps us from abundant life. We struggle with painful memories and areas of bondage; specific issues trip us up and certain relationships weigh us down.

Yet as hard as it is to understand in light of the world's suffering, God cares deeply about us and wants us free as well. *Completely free.*

Isn't that amazing? We have a legal right to that freedom. Our ransom note is paid; the deal is done. And the fact Jesus already paid freedom's price compels me to lay hold of every ounce that belongs to me. How about you? Are you provoked yet?

Allow me to spout off for a moment: I'm irked when believers say, "In light of all of the world's suffering, I'm not going to bother God with my little troubles . . ." Let me finish that sentence: ". . . so I'll keep walking through life with my head down, defeated in everything I do. I don't need to be free. I'll just be the martyr." Which, incidentally, trivializes true martyrdom. The problem with this martyr mentality is that it's a mind-set of unbelief.

If we truly are believers, then we must believe the truth that says, *It's for freedom that Christ has set us free! We must refuse to be subject to a yoke of slavery* (see Galatians 5:1). Forgive my angst, but I'm fired up about this.

One of my favorite verses is 1 Corinthians 4:20: *For the kingdom of God is not a matter of talk but of power* (NIV). If we live a life bound by unbelief, it absolutely doesn't matter if we talk a good talk. No one will believe what we say if they see we're not free. Denying or justifying bad attitudes and behaviors chains us to immaturity. Hidden sins bind us in the rusty shackles that we mistakenly think have power over us. Our only hope for freedom is to shake loose those chains and step into the light of God's truth. When we own up to our sins and our need for a Savior, He gently forgives, redeems, and restores. The path that leads from dark cell to sunlight is only a prayer away.

Satan, though, attempts to deceive us day and night. When we entertain what he has to say, we open the door to a very real enemy. Imagine inviting a known felon into your house. He's armed, he's evil, and he really doesn't care about you, yet you *let him in.* If he decided to stay for a few days or weeks, it would hugely impact how you live. In fact, you'd become a prisoner in your own home.

Lies do that. They imprison us. And then every choice we make is based on our captivity. But there's hope for the believer! God's power sets us free. God's power changes lives. God's power transforms families and communities. Our path to freedom is paved with truth, it points to peace, and it leads to abundant life. Freedom requires honesty about our fears and insecurities. It requires replacing those wretched lies with the beautiful, freeing truth of God's Word.

What you're after is truth from the inside out. Enter me, then; conceive a new, true life. (Psalm 51:6 MSG)

Sandana was only a child, yet God worked through her to change her community's social climate. God used Sandana's courage to free her as well as those she loved, and even some she barely knew.

You are a mighty woman of God, and He has a great plan for you—a plan that goes beyond personal comforts and small dreams; a plan to live free and to help secure the freedoms of others. Yours is an important destiny, a life-changing call. God's highest and best will for you involves a plan that will deeply affect your life and the lives of those you are destined to bless. They're hoping you'll have the courage and conviction to step up to all you were created to be and to accomplish.

He has anointed and appointed you for such a time as this.

Father in heaven,

I worship You today! Thank You for being the God of all comfort, the God of all hope. Thank You for patiently bearing with my fears and insecurities. I want to be done with such things! Give me courage like little Sandana. I want to stand on the side of truth and be strong in the face of evil. Bless me with more of You! Provoke me to freedom! Keep me in the center of Your will. Keep me walking toward my promised land!

And now I pray, pour out Your blessings upon Sandana and her community. Heal and restore them from all they've suffered. Help us all step up to our high calling in Christ Jesus. Give us eyes to see, ears to hear, and a courageous heart to do Your will. In Your precious name, I pray. Amen.

No study questions today

1

Recovering Lost Territory

You have allowed me to suffer much hardship, but you will restore me to life again and lift me up from the depths of the earth.
—Psalm 71:20

Without God, we cannot. Without us, God will not.[1]
—Augustine

My mother taught me never to put my elbows on the table. But there in the restaurant, I did it anyway. As I rested my forearms on the table, I leaned over my salad as if to say that the lunch part of our time together was beside the point.

My friend was as engaged as I. We talked about God's power to restore and renew. "I've seen God do amazing things in my life, but I feel as though I've only scratched the surface with what He wants to do. Do you ever feel that way?" Sheri asked.

"Yes. Absolutely!" I replied. Then I picked up a napkin and held it for Sheri to see. "Pretend this napkin represents my life. I started out with a trusting heart and a concern for other people." I tore a piece of the napkin and tossed it on the table. "But when I was a child, I learned that my grandpa died of a brain hemorrhage from a severe beating he endured in the inner city. His story and others made me afraid to go downtown."

I tore another piece. "And when I was young, teenage boys

pinned me down and took advantage of me. I lost my voice and my sense of value." I tore another piece. "When I was young, I dreamed of using my life to help others, but then a group of older boys beat me up. That was the day my fear grew and my heart shrank." I tore another piece of paper and tossed it on the table; it landed on my salad.

One by one, I watched pieces of my heart flutter to the table as I described to Sheri all of the painful memories that had shrunk my world. With tears streaming down my cheeks, I held up what was left of my napkin—a tiny remnant—and with a trembling voice said, "I want my land back!

> Follow justice and justice alone, so that you may live and possess the land the Lord your God is giving you. (DEUTERONOMY 16:20 NIV)

"My conviction is the size of this whole table, yet my courage is as small as this torn bit I hold in my hand. I feel a huge disconnect between what God has promised and what I experience! I was created to live an abundant life, but the Enemy has managed to lie, cheat, and steal it from me. I want my land back! And I want to help other women to recover their land and to restore their heart."

Teary-eyed, my friend Sheri reached across the table, squeezed my arm, and said, "I don't know what to say except this: I have to go home and spend some time with God. I too have some land to recover."

Has the Enemy bullied you off of your "property"? Has he used intimidation to keep you from laying hold of all God has promised you? Maybe you've lost "land" in the area of relationships or health or finances. Maybe you've lost trust or peace or security. Though many believe otherwise, God cares deeply about every loss and injustice; He is in the restoration business. Maybe the land God wants to restore involves your identity or your ability to embrace hope.

Jesus says, "Don't give up! I'm about to do great things in and through you! Look up! You are Mine and I love you! Keep on believing. Keep on walking!"

Put your hope in the Lord. Travel steadily along his path. He will honor you by giving you the land. You will see the wicked destroyed. (Psalm 37:34)

Has your holy tenacity waned a bit? Begin by thanking God for the blessings you enjoy and the land you currently possess. Walk the boundaries of your home and count every square inch a treasure. Look at the pictures on your wall. They're yours. Trace the outline of the windows that allow you to look out where the birds sing and the sun shines. If you have children, place your hand on their heads and whisper a prayer of thanks. Next time you go to church, look around. Be amazed that you are free to come and go as you please.

Notice your portion of land; be thankful for it. Simply by expressing your gratitude to God out loud, you'll bring courage to your heart and strength to your soul. When you start counting your blessings, you'll feel the wind in your sails once again.

Always be thankful. In *every* situation. No matter how you feel at the moment, you're always surrounded by God's mercy and goodness. We won't fully appreciate all these treasures until we're in heaven, looking down on the time line of our life.

On that day, I know I'll gasp as Jesus tells me about all of the ways He intervened on my behalf. I'll be speechless, moved to tears by all of the times He rescued me from a sin or a scenario that could have cost me my life or my ministry.

But even now you can point to tangible ways He has worked on your behalf and say, "He did that. My God provided that for me. It's because of Him that I'm in this house, or that I'm married to this man, or that I still have my best friend, or that my child still lives." God has come through for you and me in ways too many to count.

> Be thankful in all circumstances, for this is God's will for you who belong to Christ Jesus. (1 Thessalonians 5:18)

Gratitude awakens our heart to the movement of God around us. He loves to give good gifts to His children, and He has been good to you and me.

Ask Him to awaken your heart to bigger faith and broader horizons. Pray too that He'll increase your awareness of those who need fresh faith and newfound hope. Look around. Whisper a prayer for wisdom. Open your ears. God is breathing. God is moving. And He'd love for you to join Him.

When every past hurt and offense are covered in Calvary love, victory happens. When every fear is conquered by God's perfect love, freedom happens. And when freedom happens, we live and breathe and impart freedom to almost everyone we meet.

Now look around at your sphere of influence. Do you know someone who has been bullied out of her inheritance? Or someone for whom you can stand in the gap? Write a letter, bring a meal, say a prayer, or send some money. Do something today for someone who needs an advocate.

Ask for more! Expect more! Instead of asking for a drink of water, prepare for God's raging river to sweep you off your feet and take you to your next place of promise! Please Him by raising your level of belief and expectation. May you be like a tree, planted by Living Water, bearing fruit in each season *without fail.* And may whatever you do prosper! May you be like a well-watered garden and an ever-flowing spring receiving His blessings and sending them out again (see Psalm 1 and Isaiah 58:11).

Precious Lord,

You are all I need. Forgive me for hiding, for making excuses, and for believing a lie when I should have believed You. Give me a hunger for wholeness and restoration; help me to want it as much as You want it for me. Show me the land You want to recover for me. Give me boldness to believe that You want to increase my heart and my horizon. I know the Enemy wants to steal it from me. I will trust You, Lord, and I will not be afraid. Lead me to the next place You have for me.

And now, Lord, I pray for the twenty-seven million slaves held in captivity. Hear their cry and answer their prayers! Let them feel Your presence and bring them an advocate. For those who are in desperate need, Lord, please be their provider. And for those who put themselves in harm's way to do Your work, surround them with an abundance of protection and provision. Finally, I ask that You would use me today. Open my eyes to the needs around me. Grant me faith to see Your Kingdom come right where I live. Lead me to those You've appointed me to bless. In Your precious name, I pray. Amen.

initiate your freedom

1. Read Psalm 37:23 and ponder its truth. God cares about every detail of your life. Have you surrendered some "land" God wants to restore? Explain.

2. Write a prayer reflecting your desire for freedom in a particular area. Find a Scripture that matches your situation; write that promise at the end of your prayer. Tuck the prayer in your Bible and come back to it again and again, bringing your request to God until freedom becomes your reality.

3. Think about a time you set a goal and worked hard to reach it. What obstacles did you overcome? Write them down. What positives came out of this challenge? Write them down. Those attributes will come in handy on this journey.

4. Ultimately God brings the victory, but we most certainly work alongside Him in this battle. That's why He provided us with armor. Read Ephesians 6:10–18 and then reread it.
   - God gives very clear directives in this passage. List them one by one (e.g., "Be strong in the Lord's power ").
   - Think over the various pieces of armor and list the one you're least comfortable "wearing" (e.g., breastplate of righteousness, sword of the Spirit).
   - Time for growth! Determine to study why each piece of armor is necessary. Ask the Lord for more insight. Search the Word for His promises and provision. Educate yourself. Put on the whole armor of God!

5. Read Psalm 41:1–2. Take a minute to look inward. In what ways have you regarded the weak? Write them down. Why do you suppose God connects your concern for the weak with His promise to protect you? Share your thoughts.

"God works in wonderful ways—he chooses the weakest and does great things through them. My experience with IJM has taught me that I can put my best effort in everything and leave the rest to God, knowing that He will surely honor my efforts."

—A., ATTORNEY, IJM SOUTH ASIA

 **2**

Embodying Truth
and Courage

*Truth springs up from the earth, and righteousness smiles
down from heaven.* —Psalm 85:11

Justice is truth in action. [1] —Joseph Joubert

"He hasn't asked for me *in over a month! And you want me to
approach him now? Don't you know I could die for that? Everyone knows that
to approach the king without an invitation invites certain death with only one
exception: if he extends his royal scepter. But how will I know what his response to me will be? You don't know what you're asking for!"*

*Mordecai huddled over the message in his hands. Without lifting his head
he peered around to see if anybody was watching him. Line by line he read
Esther's words. Then he wrote furiously this reply:*

*"Don't think that because you live in the king's house you're the one Jew
who will get out of this alive. If you persist in staying silent at a time like this,
help and deliverance will arrive for the Jews from someplace else, but you and
your family will be wiped out. Who knows? Maybe you were made queen for
just such a time as this."* [2]

Esther was an orphan in a foreign land. When both of her parents died, her cousin Mordecai took her away from her homeland
and cared for her. She had no say about where she would live.

No say. No choice.

Then one day Esther was again whisked away without her permission. She had no right to say, "Yes, that would be nice," or "No, I'm not comfortable with that." What would *that* do to your sense of security? If someone moved me out of my home to a new location—and I had no say in the matter—my confidence and security would be turned upside down. And that's an understatement.

Culturally this sort of thing happened back then. Actually it happens in our day too. A million times a year, at least. The difference is that most young girls today are "moved" into horrific conditions, and their change of location is not part of God's plan. Though Esther's move was uncomfortable, her new home was marked by wealth. And her change of location was part of God's plan.

Imagine the world she entered. As Esther walked into the king's palace, she stepped out of a life of poverty and into one of decadence. Right from the start, the overseer Hegai liked Esther. My guess is she wasn't as demanding as the others. Either way, she won the admiration of those around her. A certain favor surrounded this young woman of humble means.

When it was time, Esther went before the king and pleased him so much that he fell madly in love with her. She became queen, a position for which God had been grooming Esther her whole life.

Consider the magnitude of this story. God took a humble young girl and elevated her to a place of influence, but not just to redeem her past that she might relish in her new surroundings. God entrusted her with a profound opportunity to be a conduit to justice and freedom.

So it is with us.

Every once in a while, a special moment comes when—despite our fears and weaknesses—God calls us to step up to be used of Him.

Let's look a little closer at this story's significance. God has something there for us. Read this excerpt from the book *Women of the Bible*:

Subject to the foreign powers after the Exile, God's people must have felt among the weakest elements of society. But weaker even than a Jewish man exiled to a foreign land was a Jewish woman. And weakest of all would have been a young orphan of Jewish descent. God had once again employed one of his favorite methods for accomplishing his purposes; he had raised the weakest of the weak, placing her in a position of immense strategic importance.

But it had been up to Esther to decide whether she would play the part God offered. Like Moses, she chose to identify with God's people even if it meant risking her life to do so. . . . Earthly powers were at work to kill and destroy, but a heavenly power, far greater in scope, was at work to save and preserve.[3]

Think about that: *Earthly powers were at work to kill and destroy, but a heavenly power, far greater in scope, was at work to save and preserve.* Just as it is today.

At the right place and the right time (and after earnest prayer and fasting), Esther stepped before the king. He extended his royal scepter, and she was invited into his presence.

I'm sure the Devil tried to leverage Esther's misfortune as a child to convince her that her words didn't matter. The Devil does that. He convinces us that our words don't matter, because *they do.* He convinces us that we don't matter, because *we do.* Do you suppose that sly Enemy of ours saw such potential in Esther that he used her pain to provoke doubt? Has he done the same to you? Think back over the years. He always overplays his hand. How has he tried to devalue you? What lie has he tried to convince you to believe?

Esther easily could have doubted the value of her words. Yet suddenly she had a say. She had a voice. She had an opportunity to deliver a message that would change the course of the Enemy's plans. Esther knew the risk involved, a life-and-death one. But she also understood that *every* Jewish person's life was on the line if she didn't speak up. No pressure.

The king believed a lie about the Jewish people, one that would cost them dearly unless Esther alerted him to it. He had unwittingly endorsed a scheme to wipe them out.

> The Lord works righteousness and justice for all the oppressed.
>
> (PSALM 103:6 NIV)

Maybe for a moment Esther hoped she could put her head on her pillow and wait for the danger to pass. But Mordecai's words of truth shot through her denial and hit their mark. Esther stepped up and took her rightful place as a spokesperson on God's behalf for the Jewish people.

God positioned Esther, and she risked her life to speak the truth on behalf of those in need. She stepped into the moment for which He'd groomed her . . . for "such a time as this." In a short amount of time, God turned the tables on this evil plan.

The Jewish people were not exterminated that day. Haman, the man who orchestrated the wicked plan, was sentenced to die instead. *He* hung on the very gallows intended for one he intended to kill: Esther's cousin, Mordecai. When the powers of truth and courage come together, the Enemy's plan is destroyed.

It takes great courage to face a lie, and even more courage to speak the truth. You see, when you hold on to a lie, you let go of the powerful destiny God makes available for those who believe Him. Someone once said, "The Devil lies to you, God tells you the truth, but *you* are the one who casts the deciding vote." To whom will you listen? Whom do you believe? Your agreement means everything!

God has destined you for certain opportunities. He may call upon you to be acquainted with someone else's suffering. To stand in the gap and advocate for someone in need. To step up to a task for which you're not qualified (but as far as He's concerned, you're more than equipped). He's preparing you right now.

Be like Esther. Be a woman of honor, of holy confidence and humble dependence, of Kingdom passion and Calvary love. Live like Esther. Follow God's lead. Allow Him to prepare you. Believe in your divine value. And have the courage to live by the *truth* of His Word. That's the stuff of freedom.

> For the Lord loves justice, and does not forsake His saints; they are pre-served forever, but the descendants of the wicked shall be cut off. The righteous shall inherit the land, and dwell in it forever. The mouth of the righteous speaks wisdom, and his tongue talks of justice. (Psalm 37:28–30 NKJV)

Father in heaven,

Teach me more about Your heart for Your people. You are mighty to save. You are brave and wonderful. And You have Your eye on me. Help me, Lord, to walk in the kind of bold faith that pleases You. Help me to fully embrace the truth of who I am and what I'm called to. May I have the courage to face the reality of our times, to stand in the gap, and to speak the truth even when it costs me, because that's how You lived. That's how You loved. And I want to be like You.

And now, Lord, I pray for the twenty-seven million slaves in our world today. Dear Father, bring justice and freedom to these people! Bring the truth of their imprisonment to light and provoke those in authority to put an end to this crime! Give Your people the courage to stand in the gap and to prayerfully and financially support efforts to secure the freedom of these precious souls. Show me what my part is and then help me to do it. In Jesus' name, I pray. Amen.

1. Read Esther 8:11. Notice that God didn't take the battle away from the Jewish people, He just made it a winnable one. In what ways are you engaged in a battle for freedom? Remember, for the believer every battle is a winnable one.

2. Read Acts chapter 4. Why were Peter and John thrown into prison?
   • Have you ever paid a price for doing the right thing?
   • Were you able to keep a divine perspective or did you simply feel cheated? Explain.

3. Peter and John worked for the Lord and yet paid a price for it. When it came time to speak before the officials, Peter was filled with the Holy Spirit. Read verses 8–11 again and take note of Peter's courage. His faith trumped his fear.
   • Spend a moment in prayer. Ask God to enlarge your capacity for faith, courage, and conviction. Ask Him to bless you with a fresh and divine perspective.

4. Read verse 13 and take note of Peter's qualifications or lack thereof. Peter was a history maker. So were Harriet Tubman and Corrie ten Boom (both simple yet powerful women). And so are you. If you allow yourself to dream big, how can you envision changing the world?
   • Look at the last part of verse 13 and consider its application for you. The officials recognized that Peter and John had been with Jesus. Someone once asked, "If someone accused you of being a Christian, would there be enough evidence to convict you?" Take a moment to ponder your walk with God. Ask Him to fan the flame of your passion for Him.

5. Read verse 14 where Peter and John were vindicated. Do you need to be vindicated in some way? Ask the Lord to come to your aid. Give your cares to Him and take your hands off the situation. Write a prayer releasing your burden to God; date your declaration that God will indeed come through for you. Visit that entry whenever you feel your faith falter.

6. Read the rest of the chapter (verses 15–37) and marvel at the power of the living God. Ponder how faith increased, people gave generously, some were healed, and still others were fed. Kingdom life always calls us to *faith risks*, to *sacrificial giving*, to *helping others in need*, and to *boldly proclaiming the truth* of Jesus Christ. Which of these four might be a growth area for you? Be persistent in bringing this virtue before the Lord. One day you'll be strong in that area!

"I have experienced firsthand that God makes a way where there seems to be no way. . . . My testimony is that God is ever faithful and is in complete control. I have learned to completely entrust to Him our seemingly impossible tasks."

—JED, ATTORNEY, IJM MANILA

Transcending Evil and Pain

Today I have given you the choice between life and death, between blessings and curses. Now I call on heaven and earth to witness the choice you make. Oh, that you would choose life, so that you and your descendants might live!

—Deuteronomy 30:19

God, who foresaw your tribulation, has specially formed you to go through it, not without pain but without stain.[1]

—C. S. Lewis

"How is it that you're not mad at God for all you've endured? I mean, how can you love Him as you do?"

I paused, and for a moment, I was taken aback by her question. But the woman in front of me deserved an answer. She had just heard me speak and needed some clarification.

Not that I couldn't relate to being angry at God. I could. I've shaken my fist at Him. I've screamed out loud in desperation for answers. I've thrown my pillow across the room in anger. I've cried over and over again, "How long, O Lord, until You rescue me from this pain in my heart? How long do I have to wait until You heal this sickness in my body?"

Crying out to God is an essential part of authentic faith. Read the Psalms and you'll find that King David's passion is hard to miss. I'm regularly passionate in my prayers. But embracing anger to the point of holding a grudge against God, well, that's a different thing altogether.

In the midst of my seasons of great pain and disillusionment, I grew to love and fear God enough to know that I couldn't embrace an irreverent attitude for an extended period of time without losing sight of who He really was.

The woman in front of me wanted an answer, and whenever I'm asked a thought-provoking question, I whisper a prayer for wisdom before I ever open my mouth. I uttered my prayer, then stepped a little closer to the woman. I gently touched her arm and began to speak. "Yes, I've struggled in the past with anger toward God. But that was before I knew Him well. Knowing Him better has helped me to understand in the depths of my being that He's always good. *He's always good*, even when life is bad. And though I didn't feel my trials had a limit back then, I now know God set definite boundaries around them, much as He did for Job.

"Plus, I have a pretty good sense of who I would be if not for God's painful and wonderful refining work in my life. I understand with all of my heart that though God didn't deliver all of that pain and heartache to me, He in His wisdom used it to change me. Even in the midst of my hard times He showed me glimpses of His glory. I eventually understood and believed—right in the middle of my pain—that He was up to something *good*. He used the wretched pain of sickness and betrayal to confront the lies and insecurities buried in my spiritual foundation. It's as though He had to level the building to fix the foundation. I'm no longer that fearful, insecure girl I once was. I have things to do in this world, and by His grace and leading, I'm going to fulfill my call to bear much fruit and change the world."

My new friend's eyes welled with tears and we lingered together for a few more minutes. She was in the middle of the fire. She couldn't see Jesus, and she was certain that even if she did survive this trial, her heart and her perspective would still reek of smoke. She felt abandoned and alone. We prayed together and I wrapped her in a hug. I challenged her to have faith and courage in spite of how things looked or felt at the moment. I grabbed her shoulders, looked her in the eyes, and said, "You can do this! God's grace combined with your faith will get you through this! Guard your thoughts consistently. Recite His promises to you. Stand firm and God will surely deliver you in due time."

As soon as God's goodness is up for grabs, we become an easy target for despair and discouragement. The minute we doubt that God has our best interests at heart, we allow the Enemy to cast even *more* doubt on our circumstances. As he did with Eve in the garden of Eden, Satan will throw out such questions to us: "Did God *really* say . . . ?" "Are you sure that's what you heard?" "What if you heard wrong?" "What if He never comes through for you?" "Your situation is beyond hope."

In times of despair and pain, we must remember that God is always good. He passionately loves us. He is true to His Word. He keeps His promises.

Jesus intercedes for us every day, and if we look to Him, He will come through for us in His own time and own way. Which is always the best way.

Even so, terrible, horrific, unimaginable things happen to us. Why does God allow it? If He's so powerful, why doesn't He intervene? If He's so good, why doesn't He stop every wicked plan before it comes to pass?

Everyone asks these questions from time to time. Many people are offended with God because of our world's pain and suffering. These questions will not be fully answered until we see Jesus face-to-face. If I consider our world's incredible suffering in the absence of

God's presence and promises, I'm crushed beneath its weight.

But then I consider that God has called me to carry a portion of His burden for the world—and He's called you to do the same. And when I embrace His promise to strengthen me for the call, I know I can do all things through Christ who strengthens me. When God provokes me to do something for the poor, the persecuted, the slave, and the sick, I'm reminded once again of *His heart*. It's His heart that compels me to make a difference, not mine. It's His heart that provokes me to prayer, not mine.

It takes a depth of faith and a measure of understanding to see God for who He is in light of the world's condition. God knows that. And you are blessed if you wrap your heart around such a truth. *And if anyone is not offended because of Me, he is blessed* (Matthew 11:6 HCSB).

We are the ones who assign motives to God, who judge Him for not caring. And when we do that, we are perfectly wrong about Him. We want our choices. We want our way. We don't want anyone telling us what to do. We get angry when our plans fall apart. We wonder why God isn't at our beck and call. But we forget that God is God. We don't get to dictate our ways to Him. *People ruin their lives by their own foolishness and then are angry at the Lord* (Proverbs 19:3).

Furthermore, one day He will set the record straight. For now He has entrusted us with the gift of free will to do with as we choose. But our choices are not without consequence. One day every person's choices will be put through the fire. The evil man will face judgment; the righteous man will be blessed; and the apathetic man? Well, he is in for the shock of his life.

Following Christ is costly. Satan knows his doom is sure and pulls out all stops to steal, kill, and destroy. We are engaged in an all-out battle between good and evil, right and wrong, holiness and wickedness, the truth and the lie . . . and war is *never* easy.

The devil does not sleep, nor is the flesh yet dead; therefore, you must never cease your preparation for battle, because on the right and the left are enemies who never rest.[2]   —Thomas à Kempis

Although Satan is powerful, he is not in control of this world. On the contrary, Scripture says, *The earth is the Lord's, and everything in it* (Psalm 24:1).

Satan gets away with murder, yet he can be stopped. But it won't happen without us. God works through His people. *We* are the resistance against evil.

One day during a radio interview, I shared about the International Justice Mission's work on the issue of human trafficking. A caller asked me, "How can a loving God allow such horrific things to happen?" Again I whispered a prayer for wisdom. Then I said, "Since God has determined to work through His people, I think the question is not, 'How can God allow this to happen?' but rather, 'How can *we* allow this to happen?' This is happening on our watch. And we are the ones—with God's help—who need to stand in the gap."

While we are alive, God entrusts the world's problems to us. But He doesn't ask us to make gold bricks out of measly straw; He has equipped us for everything we're called to do.

In His sovereignty and according to His purpose and by His deliberate plan, He has chosen to leave humans free to experience His kingdom, through His presence, or not . . . And this does not mean that He has backed out and relinquished ownership, but that He has entrusted the earth to mankind . . . The kingdom of God will always, without fail, overpower and outmaneuver the kingdom of Satan when the kingdom of God is accessed through His people. The two kingdoms are not equal in their power, and the kingdom of darkness cannot stand against the kingdom of God.[3]

The Great News is this: In Luke 10:19, Jesus arms us with a powerful promise: *Look, I have given you authority over all the power of the enemy, and you can walk among snakes and scorpions and crush them. Nothing will injure you.*

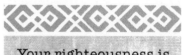

Your righteousness is like the mighty mountains, your justice like the great deep. O Lord, you preserve both man and beast.

(PSALM 36:6 NIV)

Furthermore, He promises us in Ephesians 6:16 that our shield of faith can extinguish every fiery dart the Enemy sends our way. He's given us authority over *all* of the Enemy's power; a shield of faith to block *every* fiery dart aimed at us (or those for whom we are standing in the gap). *No* weapon formed against us will prosper.

We are the resistance against the evils in this world. Wrapped in the armor of God, standing on His promises, we are called to affect change, to stand in the gap, to gain ground, and to be the hands and feet of Christ for a world in need. Satan's rule is overcome when God's Kingdom is exercised through us.

We have received the keys to heaven, keys to access all of God's available resources: *You will have complete and free access to God's kingdom, keys to open any and every door: no more barriers between heaven and earth, earth and heaven. A yes on earth is yes in heaven. A no on earth is no in heaven* (Matthew 16:19 MSG).

What does God want us to do about evil? Is there really anything one person can do? I can tell you what he doesn't want us to do—to ignore it, deny it, pretend it doesn't exist, close our hearts and minds to it, or hope it goes away by itself. He doesn't want us to appease it, placate it, compromise with it, coexist with it, justify it, excuse it, or call it by another name. In God's value system, these responses are as wicked as endorsing, cooperating with, or embracing evil. Evil will not go away by itself. It only grows more insidious by the day. It encroaches on the good, with only one goal in mind: domination and elimination of the good.[4]

Though the Enemy gets away with murder, we are made for and equipped for victory. God has called us to follow Him, to trust Him, and to stand on the side of good.

Dear and precious Lord,

You are good. You are good and Your love endures forever. Forgive me for the countless times I've doubted You and assigned wrong motives to You. You care about me. You care about every suffering soul. So much so that You ask me to join You in Your work. Help me, Lord, to trust You fully and to believe You completely.

And now, Lord, I pray for those who are right now in the clutches of evil. Bless their hearts and give them hope. Protect them in mind, body, and spirit. And God in heaven, expose and foil the plans of the Wicked One! Establish the plans of the brave souls who are acting on Your behalf. Protect them and grant their efforts success! May Your Kingdom come to every place where evil reigns! In Jesus' name, I pray. Amen.

1. Read Psalm 17:4–7 and answer the following questions:
    * In your own words, describe how obedience brings safety (verses 4–5).
    * On a scale of 1–10, how would you rate your faith level when you pray (verse 6)? No matter how you rated yourself, write a prayer asking for more faith.
    * Read verse 7 and make note of two things: the request and the declaration. Write a similar prayer with those two components.

2. Is our safety completely contingent on our behavior? Even if you're perfectly careful, is it possible for evil to cross your path? Discuss your thoughts with a friend or study group.
    * Share about a time when you were faced with evil but it did not touch you.
    * Think of a time when you know you stepped outside of God's boundaries. What happened? Can you see any ways that God still intervened despite your choices?

3. Read Psalm 37:1–6. What a powerful passage! In light of all of the evil in our world, the first verse is a bit surprising, no? Don't worry about the wicked; don't envy their success. Picture standing on the basketball court, getting ready to play a championship game, when suddenly the other team walks in the gym. They're from the land of the giants. You turn your head and swallow hard. Your coach's voice snaps you back to attention. "Look at me! Look me in the eyes! Don't worry about them. You know the drill!" Answer this for me: How often are you distracted by the giants in your land?

4. The rest of the passage is your game strategy, whether you need justice or you're fighting for it on someone else's behalf. Read the passage again.
    * I'm looking at the *New Living Translation*; your version might be different. But I see five things God calls *you* to do. List them.
    * God's promises are almost always connected to our obedience. If you do your part, God will do His. In this same passage I see five things that He has promised you. List them.

5. Read Psalm 37:37–40 and smile. God *is* a God of justice. Write a paraphrase of this passage and then follow it with a prayer of thanks to God Most High.

> "In the moments where I feel overwhelmed
> by the magnitude of the brokenness here in
> Cambodia, God gently reminds me that I have
> the privilege and opportunity to step forward
> and play my small role—and that the rest remains
> in the hands of the Master Builder."
> —NAOMI, LEGAL PROGRAM COORDINATOR, IJM CAMBODIA

4

PUTTING FEAR IN ITS PLACE

Make the Lord of Heaven's Armies holy in your life. He is the one you should fear. He is the one who should make you tremble. He will keep you safe. —ISAIAH 8:13–14

Security is mostly superstition. It does not exist in nature, nor do the children of men as a whole experience it. Avoiding danger is no safer in the long run than outright exposure. Life is either a daring adventure or nothing.[1] —HELEN KELLER

You may have heard this story already. I wrote about it in two of my other books and have spoken about it at some of my events. Those times I referred to how the incident affected me— what it did *in* me. I replay the story this time to show how God used the incident to work *through* me. Indulge me once more if you would.

When I was in fourth grade, a group of teenage boys jumped me one day as I walked home from school. They knocked me to the ground and laughed wildly as they beat me up. I screamed, cried, and covered my face with my hands as they yanked my hair, scratched my face, and took turns kicking and hitting me.

Then, out of the corner of my eye, I noticed a neighbor boy standing on the sidewalk watching the beating. I screamed at the top of my lungs, "Help meeee!"

He just stood there.

I screamed again, "Go get someone!"

He didn't move.

When the teens finished with me, they gave me one last shove and ran off. With snarled hair, a fat lip, and a traumatized soul, I made my way home. My mom wrapped her arms around me as I pressed my face against her chest and sobbed.

That night as I snuggled in the safety of my bed, I thought of the kid who stayed at a distance while I took a beating. He didn't help me, nor did he get someone who could. Instead, he just stood there. I knew, with everything within me, I never wanted to become that person.

Ever since, my heart for the marginalized and hurting affects me on many levels. I send money to organizations that minister to the oppressed. I pray consistently for the persecuted, the hungry, the human-trafficking victim, and most recently, the unjustly imprisoned.

Even as a pregnant woman, I once recklessly broke up a fight. To be more accurate, the "fight" involved a group of adolescent boys beating up one boy. As righteous indignation rose within me, I parked my car, walked right into the center of the mess, confronted the bullies, and made sure the one at the bottom of the pile got home safely. Only after I returned to my house did it occur to me that with a high-risk pregnancy, I had risked my baby's life.

Yet unfortunately, on far too many occasions, I allow fear to override my convictions. When faced with certain injustices, I freeze, feeling helpless to make an impact for good. I just *hate* it when I do that.

In the 1980s, Christian recording artist Twila Paris released a wonderful song titled "The Warrior Is a Child." That describes me completely. One minute I'm brave and bold, the next scared out of my mind. I so much want to have more faith than fear, and sometimes I do. I can't bear the thought of giving the Enemy even an inch of the land God has destined me to possess.

But my journey forward often seems so slow. For example, some people are wired for daring mission trips. The world is their oyster—or something like that. They're not instinctively afraid. But I am. I started out my young adult life with an abundance of fear and a deficit of faith. I was in the hole, so to speak, as though all of those natural-born, missions-bound international travelers started the race months, even years ahead of me. When I showed up at the starting line, they already were long gone.

My husband and I just returned from Guatemala. We had the privilege of going with a group of IJM donors to see the work IJM is doing in that country. Little did we know that our lives were about to be marked forever by God's heart for restoration and justice. What a mighty, intimate, involved God He is. Here's my journal entry written during our travels to Guatemala:

On our way to Guatemala, we have a long layover in Texas. I just finished reading the traveler's information on international travel, and specifically, on Guatemala. I guess there are about a thousand ways to be pick-pocketed or mugged, and I'm supposed to be aware of my surroundings at all times. Won't be too difficult, since I'm constantly hyperaware of potential dangers all around me. Problem is, I wasn't aware of this particular list: there's the "mustard trick" and "dropped money trick," the "escalator trick" and the "luggage trick." I'm supposed to beware of large crowds and empty alleys; I'm supposed to carry my money inside my clothes; I'm supposed to make sure Kevin walks right behind me at all times; I'm not supposed to be out at night, unless I'm with a group, but even then, it's not a good idea.

Well, now my wretched fears have surfaced and suddenly I feel very vulnerable. These kinds of journeys confront me so. Right now I feel that familiar fist in my gut and I wonder what I am doing making this trip. My own severe digestive issues make it difficult for me to eat regular American food, so how will

I fare in another country? My health is a constant struggle; international travel takes its toll even on a healthy person's body. And never mind my health, what if something terrible happens to Kevin and me? We have sons who still need us!

But I know I have to go. I want everything You have for me, Lord.

(An hour later . . .)

A few moments ago, I picked up Kay Warren's book Dangerous Surrender: What Happens When You Say Yes to God. *I love every word of this book. In fact, I just stumbled across a quote in it from Francis Fénelon; I believe it's a word for me—right here, right now. Thank You, Lord.*

Here it is:

"To want to serve God in some conditions, but not others, is to serve Him in your own way. But to put no limits on your submission to God is truly dying to yourself. This is how to worship God. Open yourself to God without measure. Let His life flow through you like a torrent. Fear nothing on the road you are walking. God will lead you by the hand. Let your love for Him cast out the fear you feel for yourself."[2]

Hmm. *Let your love for Him cast out the fear you feel for yourself.* Those words were a healing balm to my fearful soul. Amidst the chaos of the Houston airport, I set my book in my lap, looked out the window, and recommitted myself to the promise I made to the Lord to follow Him all the days of my life. I allowed my love for Him to override the fear I had for me. I knew He led me to this place; He'd be with me every step of the way. Someone once said, "If He leads you to it, He'll lead you through it."

Our trip to Guatemala was life-changing. And my fears? They amounted to exactly nothing. I can honestly say that for the majority of the trip I was more God-aware than self-aware. I saw God's influence in high levels of government and His presence in the most obscure nooks and crannies of humanity. God's vast love overwhelmed me and the work of IJM captivated me. What amazed me so was this: while I faced potential for real danger in Guatemala, I felt less fear. I'm changing! I can't even tell you how happy that makes me!

Read this great quote from IJM President Gary Haugen: "God doesn't call us to *try* to be brave, but to *train* to be brave."[3]

I'm not suggesting one has to travel internationally to run the race appointed her by God. Not everyone is called overseas. But we must find our own way to lessen the plight of humanity in the most desperate of places.

Yes, we have needs right here in our country, and it's important to tend to them. God is here, with us. But God is over there too, watching, listening, providing for, and working through any and every available soul. And He tells us in no uncertain terms to defend the orphan, to rescue the oppressed, and to stand in the gap for those with no advocate.

Modern-day slavery and sex trafficking . . . rape . . . the theft of a grieving widow's land . . . these brutal crimes are perpetrated *this very day* against millions of men, women, and children. They beckon believers to step up and do whatever it is God gives us to do.

I serve as an occasional backup host for a two-hour radio talk show called *Along the Way.* A couple of weeks ago I invited national recording artist Sara Groves to appear on the show. Here's my paraphrase of what Sara told me she says when people ask her what they can do about slavery and human trafficking: *My journey is going to be different than yours. I'm just following the bread crumbs God gives me and I follow where He leads. One step at a time, a little at a time, as God leads, I take on more responsibility to be God's hands and feet for the sake of justice. You can do the same. Just do what He says and follow where He leads.*

Perfectly said, wouldn't you agree? *My journey is different than yours.* In fact, you may be much further down the justice road than I am. After all, I am not your typical globally minded person. Yet the longer I follow Jesus, the more He leads me to faraway places and people I'll probably never meet this side of heaven. By asking God to burden my heart with His burdens, I find myself caring for those desperately in need of an advocate. Regularly I ask Him for courage and conviction to trump my wretched fears.

I strongly sense God's love and patience with me in this process of global awakening. Maybe that's because of the way I love and understand my sons. I know what it takes for them to accomplish great things. When my second son, Luke, received a B in a very difficult middle-school class, I couldn't have been more proud. I celebrated. I made lots of noise. I jumped up and down. I baked Luke his favorite snack. My heart swelled with joy because I knew how hard Luke worked to achieve that B.

> The Lord looked and was displeased that there was no justice. He saw that there was no one, he was appalled that there was no one to intervene.
> (ISAIAH 59:15-16 NIV)

Never mind the student who sat behind him in class, the one who could get a B in his sleep. For Luke to step up, fight doubt and defeat, and apply himself in a way that was difficult for him—that was downright heroic. And spiritually speaking, here's an important analogy: we're not accountable for how our accomplishments measure up to the gifted person sitting next to us. However, we *are* accountable for what *we* do with what *we've* been given. God knows how we're wired because He created us! He is well aware of His investment in us. He knows when we're lazy or too casual with these priceless gifts He's bestowed on us. He knows what it takes to step up and face fear. And when we do, He jumps up and down, makes some noise, and cheers us on every step of the way.

Christians ought not to be smothered in fear. There is a spiritual readiness, where we return to having the peace of God stand guard over our hearts and minds. What an incredible witness it is to a lost and fearful society when the Christian acts like a child of God, living under the loving sovereignty of the Heavenly Father. The Christian needs to walk in peace, so no matter what happens they will be able to bear witness to a watching world.[4]

—Henry Blackaby

Dear heavenly Father,

You take such good care of me. Forgive me for ever doubting You; You deserve my ultimate trust. Reach inside my soul and remove every lesser affection, every trumped-up fear, and every reason for not becoming all I was meant to be. Take me by the hand and lead me to the places You have for me. Transform me into someone with great inner beauty and mighty strength, and use me for Your name's sake.

And now, Lord, I pray for the millions of men, women, and children who suffer at the hands of evil people. Supernaturally intervene in their situations and show them Your presence. Help them to know Your power and Your promises. Cut off the strength of the wicked and increase the power of the godly. In Jesus' name, I pray. Amen.

initiate your freedom

1. Read Isaiah 41:10 and notice how clear God makes His exhortation. What's your part in this verse? Write it down. Who does He say He is? Write it down. And what does He promise to do for you? Write it down. Rewrite this verse into a prayer of thanksgiving to God.
2. Read Psalm 27:2–3 and imagine possessing that kind of confidence. Write a prayer expressing your desire to be driven more by faith than by fear.
3. Read Psalm 27:4 and then rewrite this beautiful verse in your words.
4. Read Psalm 27:5. Describe the variations between the words in this verse (e.g., the difference between being rescued and hidden; between being kept safe and set up high). Describe the tangible ways God has done this for you.
5. Read Romans 8:15 and honestly answer this question: In what ways do you behave like a daughter of God (totally provided for, totally cared for), and in what areas are you more like a cowering slave? Write a prayer and ask for freedom. Total freedom. Ask for the abundant life God has promised you!

"It is easy to see how God loves us through His protection of us in this dangerous environment. God always loves us first and shows that love every day. What is complicated is figuring out how to love one another as brothers and neighbors."

—IJM INVESTIGATOR, GUATEMALA

STANDING FAST
FOR FREEDOM

I will *walk in freedom for I have devoted myself to your com-*
mandments. —Psalm 119:45, emphasis mine

When we let freedom ring . . . when we let it ring from every
village and every hamlet, from every state and every city, we
will be able to speed up that day when all of God's children:
black men and white men, Jews and Gentiles, Protestants and
Catholics will be able to join hands and sing in the words of
the old Negro spiritual,
> *Free at last, free at last.*
> *Thank God almighty, we are free at last.*[1]

—Martin Luther King Jr.

Resolute: *admirably purposeful; determined; unwavering*[2]

It was well past two in the morning and a fog was start-
ing to blanket the ground as the short black woman resolutely strolled through
the rural cemetery gates. Waiting for her, among hand-carved wooden grave
markers, were about a dozen poorly dressed men and women. They had
sneaked away from the plantations and farms where they worked, some running more than six miles through the woods and across swamps to see this tiny
woman. Most of the twelve had never met each other. What bound them together was the color of their skin, the fact that the state of Maryland had

considered each of them property, and a common desire to taste freedom before they died.[3]

The tiny black woman standing before the frightened slaves was a legend even in her own time. Slaves across the country whispered stories about Harriet Tubman's exploits as a conductor for the Underground Railroad.

Born into slavery in 1820, Harriet Tubman was often whipped as a child. Imagine waking up each day only to be treated like property, living in debased conditions, always wondering if things would ever change. And then imagine trying to hang on to any shred of who you were in the constant presence of injustice and abuse. But Harriet did more than hang on. Even in captivity, she possessed dignity and inner strength.

But when Harriet heard she was to be sold to a different master, she decided to make a break for freedom. Resolutely led by God Himself, the young slave traveled hundreds of miles on foot from Maryland to Pennsylvania, braving the elements, firmly focused on becoming free. And after Harriet broke free, she went on to change the world. Harriet risked her life by going back into enemy territory again and again for the sake of those still needing rescue.

Harriet Tubman's uncommon courage was rooted in a childhood experience. One day while protecting another slave, Harriet received a violent blow to the head that nearly took her life. Suffering a coma and then seizures, Harriet took nearly a year to recover. She suffered debilitating headaches and sometimes passed out from the pain. Yet amazingly, during her blackouts (while others desperately worried about her), young Harriet received fresh visions of flying and freedom from the Lord. She actually awoke from these episodes renewed and refreshed. Though her body was scarred, Harriet's spirit *soared*.

Although Harriet couldn't read or write, she understood the strategies of war. As a result, on numerous occasions she provided intelligence for military raids on the South. Then, after the Civil War, Harriet spent her time praying and caring for wounded soldiers. She held dying men in her arms, prayed for them, and sang songs to them.

Harriet repeatedly risked her life because she'd already given it to her Lord. She was a hero in the truest sense of the word.

I picture that night in the cemetery: the frightened slaves comparing her tiny frame to the giant risk they were taking. And I imagine that for a moment some of them considered a change of heart. What if they didn't make it? Would the risk be worth it? Up to this point, Harriet had led hundreds of slaves to freedom in the dark of the night under God's watchful eyes—yet totally missed by those of the plantation owners (who, by the way, had placed a sizable bounty on her head).[4]

Harriet leaned on her rifle that night and told her frightened followers, "When I walked into Pennsylvania, I looked at my hands to see if I was the same person, now that I was free. There was such a glory over everything. The sun came like gold through the trees, and over the fields, and I felt like I was in heaven." Heaven on earth, she assured the slaves, was waiting for each of them.[5]

Though I used several sources for my information on Harriet Tubman, the story at the beginning of the chapter came from *Stories Behind Women of Extraordinary Faith* by Ace Collins. Here's another excerpt from that wonderful book:

In the 1850s, Harriet Tubman was called the "Moses of American slaves." Gaining her freedom had not been enough to satisfy her soul; she was driven to bring that freedom to as many as she could. This drive to bring freedom would be the defining thread that continued through the rest of her life. Thus, when it was unsafe for any man or woman of color to travel along across the Mason-Dixon Line, this ex-slave went back to the South time and time again to lead others through the American wilderness to freedom. She wore her shoes out on these trips, often coming within seconds of death, but she would not quit.[6]

Imagine yourself in Harriet Tubman's shoes. Fighting to be freed from deplorable conditions. Placing one foot in front of the other, putting slavery behind you. If a petite, abused slave can rise up, fight for freedom, secure the freedom of others, and change her world, so can I. And so can you.

Harriet Tubman's story reminds us that even if someone holds us captive, he cannot imprison our spirit. As believers, you and I must fiercely embrace our right to soul freedom. With the psalmist we too must declare, "*I will* walk about in freedom for *I have* sought out Your precepts" (see Psalm 119:45).

We don't have to be tall in stature to be mighty in battle. We don't have to be athletic or educated to be victorious for freedom. But we need faith and an understanding of God's ways. We must know Jesus intimately and earnestly seek His truth. We must be aware of the Enemy's strategies (he's very predictable and completely evil) and our vulnerabilities. We need a realistic handle on the measure of faith we actually possess. If we're too casual on any of these points, we'll wander into enemy territory. But if we're serious about staying in step with the Lord and doing great exploits with Him, there's no limit to what He can do through us.

Harriet Tubman modeled a fierce, resolute commitment to her freedom and the freedoms of others. Though our captivity is nothing like that of a slave, we too have freedoms worth fighting for so we might be completely whole and able to bear all of the fruit appointed to us by God! I've experienced freedom in once-captive areas of my life, and I echo Harriet's beautiful words, *There's such a glory over everything* when we are free!

But it doesn't stop with our freedom. Our release from captivity is for a much bigger purpose than our personal benefit. We too live in a day when slaves are trapped in deplorable conditions, beaten regularly, and desperate for release. Today, *this very day*, millions of people live under a constant abuse of power and are treated like garbage, with their basic human rights denied. Day and night many of them cry out to God—and their cry has reached God's ears!

What can you and I do? We can pray! When we fight for our freedom, we can fight for theirs. God works through His people, so when we speak of what God has done in our life, we can speak of their plight too. Millions of people don't know about the millions of slaves in our day, so we can become their voice.

Open your mouth and start sharing. Bring perspective to conversations. Remember these precious souls when you eat, when you give, when you pray. Ask God to keep their needs on your heart, because their needs are always on His. And let the courageous stories of those who've gone before us fuel in you a fiery passion for freedom.

If these words are true—*It is for freedom that Christ has set us free!*—then this challenge is ours —*Stand firm, then, and do not let yourselves be burdened again by a yoke of slavery* (see Galatians 5:1). May we walk forward from here

Is not this the kind of fasting I have chosen: to loose the chains of injustice and untie the cords of the yoke, to set the oppressed free and break every yoke? Is it not to share your food with the hungry and to provide the poor wanderer with shelter—when you see the naked, to clothe him, and not to turn away from your own flesh and blood? (ISAIAH 58:6-7 NIV)

"admirably purposeful, determined, and unwavering" in our pursuit to be fully free, as God intended.

Just how determined are you? How long have you existed on a smaller plot of land than God intended for you? All things are possible with God. The Bible says that if we ask Him for something in accordance with His will, we can know that we will have it (see 1 John 5:14). And be sure of this: God wants you free.

Ask for more freedom. Because she who asks, receives; she who seeks, finds; and she who knocks, finds an opened door. May you pursue every inch of land God offers you! Be free to love and live and serve and give. Be free!

Keep your eyes open, hold tight to your convictions, give it all you've got, be resolute, and love without stopping. (1 Corinthians 16:13–14 MSG)

 **_Heavenly Father,_**

Thank You for loving me. I believe that You want me free. Help me in my unbelief. I want the kind of courage Harriet Tubman had! Grant me a God-sized vision for my life. Help me to be unwaveringly resolute in my passion for freedom. You paid such a high price for the liberty of Your people; help me to lay hold of—in the highest way possible—the gift You've offered me here. Fill me anew today with fresh courage, faith, grit, and grace. I need them all to walk this journey. I love You, Jesus.

And now, Lord, I pray for the millions of slaves who suffer at the hands of brutal men and women. Bring down Your divine influence and move heaven and earth to save them! Confuse the plans of the Enemy and establish the plans of Your people. Raise up more brave souls like Harriet to lead the captives to their place of freedom. The times are desperate, Lord. Show us Your miracles once again. Let our children see Your glory at work! And show us Your approval and make our efforts successful. Yes, make our efforts successful (Psalm 90:16–17). Amen.

1. Read 1 Peter 1:13 and note the three things God asks of you:
    - *Think clearly.* What are your thoughts regarding your freedom and the freedoms of others? Do you possess a strong measure of clarity, or are you distracted by life? Maybe the enormity of today's issues is wearing you down. Write a prayer asking for a divinely renewed mind. Our whole life can be restored when we change the way we think.
    - *Exercise self-control.* With regard to your personal freedom, what enslaves you? Food? Shopping? Others' opinions? In what areas do you need true freedom? Remember, self-control is a fruit of the Spirit, not something to be mustered by yanking up your bootstraps. Draw near to the Lord, and by the power of the Holy Spirit, start exercising self-control today.
    - *Look forward.* To what extent are you hopeful about the future? The Bible says that even in hard times, we'll have more than enough. All of God's promises are "yes" and "amen"! Do you spend too much time looking at your past? Or maybe you're weighed down by the present. Start looking up. Let God lift your chin and open your eyes to see the wondrous works of His hands. Get a vision for your next place of promise. Be strong. Be courageous. Look forward.
2. Read Jeremiah 29:11 and answer the following question: On a scale of 1–10, where would you rate your faith with regard to this promise?
3. Read John 10:10 (NKJV) and describe in your words what "life abundantly" looks like for you.
4. Read Hebrews 12:1–3 (NKJV). This passage is rich with meaning! Stop right now and imagine the cloud of witnesses cheering you on. You have heaven's attention! Your choices matter!
    - What in your life hinders your spiritual progress?
    - Is there a besetting sin with which you need to deal?
    - Are you clear on the race God has marked out before you? If not, spend some time with the Lord and get your marching orders.
    - Consider the endurance of Jesus, *who for the joy set before Him endured the cross* (verse 2). You were the joy set before Him. He endured because of you. Pause for a minute and embrace your incredible value.
    - What in life makes you weary? Next time you feel that way, come

back to this passage. Ponder the cloud of witnesses and smile. Remember Jesus' sacrifice and endurance, and be brave. Fix your eyes on Jesus and refuse to give up. God has more for you.

"I have enjoyed seeing how God is using what we would consider to be ordinary, everyday people to do His extraordinary work. I feel blessed to be a part of a team of people that has the power to change the world because they come together in Christ's name."
—Karen, intern, IJM Cambodia

RECLAIMING
YOUR IDENTITY

God, your God, chose you out of all the people on Earth for himself as a cherished, personal treasure.

—DEUTERONOMY 7:6 MSG

For however devoted you are to God, you may be sure that he is immeasurably more devoted to you.[1]

—MEISTER ECKHART

"Will you sign my book?"

The crying woman stood in front of me, hiding her face with hair that hung forward like heavy drapes darkening a room. I wanted to see her eyes, but she wouldn't look up. I came around the table, touched her shoulder, and asked, "Can I pray with you? Can I talk with you?" Seemingly bothered by her display of emotion, she just shook her head, indicating she wanted our encounter to be brief. I rubbed her arm, wished her well, and then told her I'd be around for a little while longer in case she changed her mind. She nodded, turned around, and walked out the door. I went back to signing books.

After the event ended, my assistant and I packed up my book table and we said our good-byes. As I walked out of the double doors, I noticed the same woman, head down, leaning against a wall. I stepped toward her. "Can we talk now?" I asked. With tears streaming down her face, the woman choked out, "Do . . . do any of your books deal with regret? Do you have anything to say to someone who has wasted her life and thrown away the gifts God gave her?" Then before I had a chance to reply, she shook her head "no" as if to answer her own question.

I stepped in close, and we spent the next twenty minutes in a powerful exchange. The woman who stood before me was only in her late twenties. Yet she was saturated in regret over squandering money, hooking up with questionable people, and making rotten choices. Her life, she felt, was at a dead end; she had no hope for her future. Through sobs this exhausted, overwhelmed young woman said, "Even if God forgives me, I don't think I can forgive myself. And even if I did, I'm still stuck. How do I recover what I've thrown away?"

I needed God's divine influence for the need before me, so I whispered a prayer for wisdom before I opened my mouth. "I'd like to pray for you if I could," I said. Then I put my arm around my sweet friend and asked God to make Himself real to her. To heal her. To refresh her. Suddenly I had the most beautiful picture in my mind and I knew what God wanted me to say.

I opened my eyes, grabbed her shoulders, and said, "God has a plan for you! I saw it! You're going to minister to girls in their late teens. You're going to be honest about where you've been and what you've done. You're going to challenge them to make choices that line up with God's beautiful call on their lives. And you know what? When you get to heaven, God won't be looking at all of the years you squandered or the sins you committed. Those will be out of His sight, out of His memory. But He will see *all of the years you recovered* for young girls who otherwise would have given themselves in unholy ways. Your squandered years will pale in comparison to all of the years of godly fruit produced by those to whom God calls you. You have the opportunity to take the lessons from your mistakes and reinvest them. That's good stewardship. That's being faithful with every shred of opportunity God sends your way. Can you picture it?"

My friend smiled through her tears. "*Me?* Do you really think God could use my messes to benefit others? I've been so beaten down that the thought of turning them around for good never occurred to me."

This young woman had lost her her sense of identity in Christ. Yet from heaven's perspective, she was always valuable. That night in the church foyer, she recovered her sense of great value, profound purpose, and divine identity. And the cloud of witnesses shouted their applause.

> I know that the Lord secures justice for the poor and upholds the cause of the needy. (PSALM 140:12 NIV)

Here's an excerpt from my book *The Uncommon Woman*:

When we understand that we were created for His beautiful purpose, our eyes become more focused on what matters. We become enveloped in His relentless love for us, and we get passionate about where He is taking us. We expect to encounter a few bumps along the way, but we finally believe that bumps, bruises, and deep valleys are not defining factors for us. Yes, they mark our journey and shape us into beautiful women, but they do not have the power to diminish our value.[2]

Though I've only traveled internationally a handful of times, I've learned something that may surprise you. In many developing countries, it's common for young boys and girls to receive no birth certificate and have no knowledge of when or where they were born. On a couple of different occasions, I've met young girls who didn't know their birthday, so they just picked a date.

In America, middle-school girls huddle together and make fun of the poor girl whose clothes are outdated or ill fitting. In other parts of the world, a young girl is looked down on if she doesn't own a birth certificate. Even when I try to put myself in the shoes of these young children, I can hardly fathom the things they go without. Imagine not knowing the exact day of your birth, or who was there when you were born. Worse yet, imagine having no earthly idea who your parents are.

Of course one doesn't have to live in a developing country to not know your parents. But consider the things that *are* in place in our world. Most of us have parents and friends who love us. We have rights as a citizen of this country. We are recognized as an employee or an employer or a student or a stay-at-home mom. We are acknowledged in a plethora of ways because we have already made our mark on the world. Our life is filled with associations and experiences that point to our existence. And if necessary, we have a chance to begin again.

But for those in slavery today, their experiences tell them they're nothing but worthless pieces of property. Every new day reminds them they don't matter. They toil relentlessly. They are inhumanly used and horrifically abused. There are no birthday parties for these priceless souls. No celebrations. No invitations to someone else's party. No Tuesday morning aerobics class with friends. No Thursday morning Bible study at church. No hobbies. No dreams, really, except for the dream of freedom that some dare not even consider for fear of profound disappointment.

We are so blessed! We have so much already going for us—time and space in which to live and breathe and move. I challenge you, dear friend, to rediscover who you are, with God's help. You have the opportunity to be fully free, so go after it. And remember this: Though your sins and accomplishments, associations and experiences shape you, they do not define you. God does. And He is perfectly in love with you and me.

 **_Precious Lord,_**

Show me what part of my identity
You want to recover for me. Help me
to understand the fullness of what You
mean when You say that You want me to be free. Even
though I've made my share of mistakes, I am totally loved
by You. And even though others may see me in a different
light, Yours is the only light that matters. I want to walk
in Your presence as I live here on earth. I want to use the
freedoms I enjoy to be more like You. I want my face to
reflect Your glory and Your grace. Shine Your light on me
and set me totally free.

And now, Lord, I lift up my sisters and brothers
who are, at this moment, desperate for freedom. I think
of all the fun things I get to do, and my heart aches over
their captivity. Right in the midst of their plight, bring
swift answers to prayers, sunny days, a lighter load,
and relief from their pain. And finally, Lord, bring
freedom. I ask, and I'll keep asking. Bring freedom to
every slave alive today. In Your name, I pray. Amen.

1. Read Hosea 2:14–15 (if possible, I'd love for you to read this passage in the *New Living Translation*).

   • Verse 14 speaks to a renewed love and intimacy. Where are you at right now in your relationship with Jesus? What words would you use to describe your interactions? Even if you have a solid faith walk right now, hear Him calling, *Come away, My beloved. I want more of you, your heart, and your affections. Let's walk together with greater intimacy.* Can you hear it? Write a prayerful response to this invitation.

   • Verse 15 speaks of God's restoring power and His ability to turn our desperation into hope and opportunity. How do you need to be restored? Write it down. Remember the woman's story at the beginning of the chapter? In what tangible ways do you envision your battle wounds becoming opportunities (and a door of hope)?

   • Look at the end of verse 15. To the extent that we "give ourselves" to God we will know divine freedom. He's already broken the chains that bind us but we need His strength to step out of them. Write a faith-filled prayer declaring that you walk in step with Jesus and are free from your captivity.

2. Read Psalm 139:1–6 and consider this: Why would God—the most majestic power in the universe—make such a point to be so intimately acquainted with you and your journey? Answer this question as best you can.

3. Read Psalm 139:7–10 and answer this: Are you ever out of God's sight? Does He ever consider you an incidental speck in a vast solar system? Based on this passage, defend your value. Write your thoughts.

4. Read Psalm 139:11–18 and embrace this: Every detail of your life matters to God. Every cell, every nerve, every fear, every hope, every dream. Look at the sky right now; smile and say out loud: "I embrace this truth. I am the object of God's great love and affection." Write a prayer of thanksgiving for God's great attention to detail.

5. Read Psalm 139:19–22 and pause for a moment. Because these verses seem to jerk us out of the beautifully poetic language used in the preceding verses, they are easily passed over. Most of us don't associate with murderers or other evil people. But our friends in slavery suffer at the hands of evil people. Think about the little girls scared out of their minds at the thought of being raped for the first time (and the second, and the third, and so on). They suffer at the hands of the most debased people alive. God hates what these people are doing. Pray! Ask God to foil the plans of the wicked ones and to establish the plans of His righteous ones (see Psalm 75:10).

6. Memorize Psalm 139:23–24. Pray this prayer as often as you think about it. Be humble and open to God's discipline and direction in your life. Always remember that He disciplines those He loves. Your identity is secure.

"I long to see girls who were brutalized, girls who have issues of trust, girls with no hope whatsoever being restored to wholeness, and secure in the knowledge that they have a hope and a future."
—MURIELLA, CASEWORKER, IJM SOUTH ASIA

Believing God Is True to His Word

Maite's* Story

You have allowed me to suffer much hardship, but you will restore me to life again and lift me up from the depths of the earth. —Psalm 71:20

Wherever there is a human being, there is an opportunity for kindness.[1] —Seneca

When Maite* was two years old, her mother died. She never knew her father. Because she was orphaned at an early age, Maite's young life was marked more by losses than gains. Her sense of belonging and identity died with her mother. She had no family, no education, and no understanding of how beautiful and treasured she was.

A middle-aged woman and her son took Maite in and gave her a home. Well, sort of. They used Maite to do all of the dirty work around the house. They worked her like a slave. They abused her physically; she bore the scars to prove it. The then-adult son repeatedly molested this young girl and his knowing mother did nothing to stop him. Maite's new life was no life at all.

One day an internationally known ministry came to work with the poor in Maite's area. Maite connected with one of the workers.

*Not her real name

Then she took a mighty risk. Grabbing the worker's arm and pulling her close, Maite told the worker of her terrible home life and begged to be rescued. The ministry worker knelt on the ground, looked in Maite's eyes, and said, "I'm not in a position to rescue you, but I know someone who is. I won't give up on you."

Maite's new friend contacted the IJM Guatemala field office and informed a social worker of Maite's situation. This time it was the ministry worker's turn to take a risk. One particular day, she knocked on Maite's front door, greeted her guardian, and convinced the woman to allow Maite to go with her to lunch. Surprisingly the guardian allowed the two to go. Maite and the woman made their way to a local McDonald's where an IJM social worker waited to meet them. During lunch Maite bravely shared her story. She rolled up her sleeves to show them the scars on her arms from past abuse. She explained how they kept her out of school, used her as a servant, and refused to feed her for not working hard enough. Maite begged these women to take her out of this home.

The IJM social worker leaned toward Maite and said, "I have to do some investigating. I can't just take you out of your home. But I promise I will not forget you. I will do my homework and then come for you. You'll hear from me again."

From that day on, every time someone knocked at the door, Maite ran to open it, hoping IJM had come. Daily she wondered, *Will* today *be the day I'm rescued?*

One day there was a knock at the door. When Maite opened it, the very social worker who had promised she wouldn't forget Maite stood there. Maite's day of deliverance had arrived. IJM arranged for Maite to live at a wonderful aftercare home where young girls are loved, nurtured, educated, and prepared to thrive as Christian women in society. Maite was welcomed with open arms and ad-justed well to her new surroundings.

This past year in East Guatemala, a competition of sorts was held, a forum for young people to give speeches on human rights issues specifically related to violence against children. Brave Maite enrolled in the competition and signed up to give a speech. Every candidate was sponsored by his or her school. Every candidate, that is, except Maite. Before moving to the children's home, Maite had received no formal education; the other candidates were coached on giving speeches. Not Maite. But no matter, she still had something to say.

Unfortunately, Maite's application was denied because she had no birth certificate. You see, you have no rights if you don't exist.

Thankfully, the workers at the girls home intervened on her behalf and made this case: "Yes, it's true that Maite doesn't have a birth certificate, but isn't that precisely why she *should* participate in this competition? She is qualified to be *in* this competition because she has lived *through* the very issues to be addressed." The judges finally agreed to allow Maite into the competition, and she represented the school

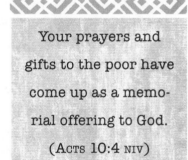

Your prayers and gifts to the poor have come up as a memorial offering to God. (Acts 10:4 niv)

in the orphanage where she lived. Maite had a new family and they were all cheering for her.

Though she hadn't received the same educational opportunities as many of the other children in the competition, Maite understood the definition of human rights because most of hers had been violated. She stood in front of the audience and the judges, and shared a compelling message. Maite won third place at the state level, which now qualified her to compete nationally.

The ride up the mountain was a bumpy one. The bus jerked right, then left, barely missing the curb or a tree or a cluster of people walking along the roadside. Normally these little details would have demanded my attention, but I refused to feel fear and instead set my eyes and ears on Pablo, IJM Guatemala's field office director. He stood with his back to the front window, facing our team, holding on to the seats while the bus jerked back and forth. As he shared Maite's story, I was captivated. But what he said next almost knocked me out of my seat.

In his thick Spanish accent Pablo said, "We're making a special trip today. You see, Maite has no birth certificate and it's something she's always wanted. Through hard work and God's mighty intervention, we tracked down Maite's baptism record from a Catholic church. Based on that date, we got her records from a local hospital, and then we confirmed a birth date and secured a legal document declaring Maite's existence. I have in my hand Maite's birth certificate. Today we deliver a great gift to this little girl." We gasped at the news and felt honored to be along for the ride.

The bus pulled up to the children's home. One by one the team members exited and looked around. We were taken by how clean, peaceful, and orderly this place was. Armed with piñatas, candy, coloring books, and treats, we excitedly showered gifts on the forty young girls who lived there, most of whom had been sexually abused.

First our team met with the director and the social worker. Speaking through a translator, we asked about the girls, the home, and the way they all lived together. When our conversation died down, Pablo pulled out a manila envelope and sat next to the director. In his humble, gentle way, he explained the envelope's contents. He talked about the hand of God and IJM's hardworking team. Then he said, "I give you Maite's birth certificate."

Right away the director's hands went to her face and she started to cry. She stood up, pointed to all of us, and said, "Do you know what this means? Do you know what this means? This means identity! This means citizenship! This means rights! This means a future and a hope! Not having a birth certificate steals your identity. And repeatedly steals from you. Let me tell you, the girls in this home know who has one of these and who doesn't. This little girl has so much potential, and now she has the means and rights to accomplish everything God has for her!"

I had one hand on my stomach and the other hand on my heart. I couldn't breathe. I was struck by how much we take for granted. I praised God and asked Him to forgive me all at the same time.

Maite's story reminds me of the importance of our spiritual citizenship. Our heavenly citizenship gives us identity, rights, a hope, and a future. God's provision gives us means to accomplish all He intends for us. And let me tell you, the angels and the demons know which souls belong to Jesus, and which lost souls are still searching for their identity in all the wrong places. We who belong to Jesus *must* know who we are because we've been given so, so much, and we have so, so much to accomplish in this life.

We spent the afternoon running relays, playing tag, and jumping around with forty young girls who clearly were cared for and loved. While I didn't speak their language, I kissed each one on the top of her head. We giggled, raced around, and made hand motions in order to communicate. After the last foot race, we gathered in a huge circle, about sixty of us in all. One little girl stepped forward to give us a special message. Through a translator she thanked us for the festive day. She then said, "God loves us and has a plan for us. We are happy and cared for here. We thank you for spending the day with us. God bless you and keep you safe."

After the game time, the director called Maite inside with the rest of the IJM team and we watched as Pablo presented her with her birth certificate. Most of us didn't understand what Pablo was saying, but the more he talked, the bigger she smiled. When Pablo finally handed over Maite's proof of existence, there wasn't a dry eye in the room. Maite clutched her birth certificate as though it was the most priceless treasure on earth.

Maite's life, her soul, her story . . . they matter. That young girl took risks to recover her identity and she has it. She knows who she is now.

Her story has never been hidden from God, and neither has yours. Every nook and cranny of your existence, every mishap and misstep, Jesus knows about them and loves you completely. You are treasured. You have girlfriends all over the world whom you've never met, but you'd love them if you did. Allow your heart to be knitted together with theirs. Enlarge your heart to include people who long for the freedoms you enjoy. And for His name's sake, press on, take risks, and recover every shred of who God intended you to be.

Watchful Father,

Thank You for Maite's story. Thank You for my story. I pray this with all of my heart: Give me more courage! More freedom! Grant me an increased capacity to know Your love. May I never be defined by what I've lost in this life. No, may I only be defined by what I've gained in You! Mark my life with boldness and belief. Fill me up with joy and peace. Enlarge my perspective and increase my sphere of influence. Give me a love for those I've yet to meet.

And now, Lord, I pray for every soul whose identity has been lost. Holy Lord, bless IJM and similar or-ganizations that work tirelessly to bring life and free-dom to those in need. Stretch out Your hand and move mountains on their behalf. Give birth certificates to those who desperately need them; pour out Your truth to those who believe a lie; and minister freedom to those who are held captive. Forgive me for how much I take for granted, Lord. Remind me to be thankful with each new day. In Jesus' name, I pray. Amen.

No study questions today

EMBRACING OTHERS' SUFFERINGS

Truth is nowhere to be found, and whoever shuns evil becomes a prey. The Lord looked and was displeased that there was no justice. He saw that there was no one; he was appalled that there was no one to intervene. —ISAIAH 59:15–16 NIV

A gospel that doesn't acquaint itself with the sufferings of others, is not the Gospel.[1] —SARA GROVES

As I rolled over in bed, I felt strangely disoriented by sounds coming from the kitchen downstairs. *Where am I? Am I in my own bed?* My brain was foggy and my eyelids felt as though they were made of iron.

Again I heard noises coming from downstairs. *I am home. Is Kevin still home?* Normally I'm up before my husband, but a terrible dream had kept me from waking up at my usual hour. I whipped back the covers and raced down the stairs right into his arms. "Oh, my goodness. You're still here. I'm still here," I whispered. "Thank you, Jesus." I couldn't hold Kevin any tighter.

"What's going on, honey? Are you okay?" Kevin asked while trying to peek at my face. I hung on a little while longer, then looked up at him. "I had a terrible dream last night. It was so real that I was surprised to wake up from it."

"Tell me," he urged without loosening his grip.

I looked around for a moment, caught up in the sight of my home and my big strong husband standing in front of me. Then I pulled him tighter, buried my face in his chest again, and began to explain: "You and I were ministering in the Middle East with a group we just met, although some in the group apparently were pretending to be Christians. One day you and I walked on a main thoroughfare, holding hands.

"We met a large crowd headed in the opposite direction. The current of people came between us and we lost hold of each other. In the scuffle I lost my purse. At that moment, someone grabbed me and brought me to an apartment that happened to belong to two of the girls in our group who were pretending to be Christians.

"I frantically looked around and asked, 'What am I doing here? I need a phone, I don't have my purse!' The girls played dumb, as though they didn't know why I was there or why all of the phones in their apartment were missing. I kept asking, 'Why are you doing this? I need to call my husband!' They proceeded to get ready to go out for the evening. They each carried a couple of strange books in their arms and were on their way to a meeting.

"As they prepared to leave, I asked, 'Why are you leaving me here?' One girl glanced toward the living room. There sat a beefy man in a recliner, a briefcase open at his feet.

"I found a phone and quickly called your cell phone. And at that precise moment, a phone in the briefcase rang. Several more times the phone at my ear rang in sync with the phone in the man's briefcase. Your phone was routed to his phone! I suddenly looked at the man and somehow realized he had been tapping our phones and trailing us for some time.

"While looking into his briefcase the man said out of the side of his mouth, 'They pay big money for blondes.' Instantly I realized that I was about to be trafficked! I swallowed hard. My skin got hot.

I started to sweat. My heart raced. I froze with fear. Every nerve in my body felt pain and terror."

I then looked up at Kevin and continued, "I've known fear in my life, but nothing close to this. The sounds of you knocking around in the kitchen this morning pulled me out of a nightmare that had completely swallowed me alive."

My husband wrapped his arms around me again and prayed a prayer of protection over me. After he left for work, I dragged myself to my spot on the couch where I have my quiet time every morning. Normally this is the sweetest part of my day. But this particular morning, I felt as though the Enemy had pummeled me.

The Lord led me to read Psalm 27, which was perfect for what I was feeling. If you struggle with fear, read the whole chapter. Here are the first two verses:

> The Lord is my light and my salvation—so why should I be afraid? The Lord is my fortress, protecting me from danger, so why should I tremble? When evil people come to devour me, when my enemies and foes attack me, they will stumble and fall. (Psalm 27:1–2)

Though God's Word comforted me, it troubled me too. *What about the millions of girls, Lord? What about them?* A few years ago I watched some undercover footage of very young girls in a brothel all lined up, all offered to the next paying customers (who were in fact undercover IJM investigators). The head pimp bragged about one little girl in particular who was new to the brothel. "She a virgin. She no been with a man yet. More for her." He charged more for the little girl who was yet to be raped by a paying customer.

The camera panned over to the little girls. Even though they were threatened to smile for the customers, the horror in their eyes was unmistakable—especially in the eyes of the one who had just arrived there. As long as I live, I'll never forget the look on her face.

Her mouth attempted a smile but none would come. Her terrified eyes betrayed her. With her hands at her side and fear all over her face, she stood frozen next to the more "experienced" little girls. She was literally stuck in a place that was hell on earth.

That little girl was someone's girl. She was beautiful and sweet and belonged in a warm bed with a teddy bear and a night-light.

Not one of these girls belonged in such a ghastly place.

As I sat on my couch with my Bible in my lap, I bowed my head and thought of the frightened little girl whose face I cannot forget. I thought of the countless other little girls held captive right now who should be safe in a loving home. I remembered the sheer terror I felt in my bones just hours ago. I had—in a small way—experienced a moment of their daily, unfathomable nightmare.

While I believe my dream was the Enemy's attempt to paralyze me with fear, somehow God used that wretched nightmare to help me relate—on a deeper level—with His little girls held captive. In a whole new way, their plight got under my skin.

My fear compelled me to address their fear with a fire in my prayers and a fresh passion in my actions. Their plight progressively changes the way I live and give and pray and invest my time.

Countless people are tortured, ripped off, betrayed, and abused. These precious souls are desperate for someone to care. And according to the verse at the beginning of this chapter, God is appalled that so few do.

But in one way or another, we're all ripped off or inflicted with pain, betrayal, fear, or injustice. When we allow our past and current plights to fuel our prayers, we can leverage them for the sake of the suffering.

Maybe you struggle with chronic health issues and can only dream about being able to bounce through your days with consistency and strength. Use your suffering for the Kingdom's sake. Think about the AIDS victim who lives in a cardboard box under a tree, just waiting to die. Pray for her. Read about her. Be an advocate for her.

Or perhaps you're in dire financial straits; I know we have been. Think for a moment of how the heavy weight of that burden presses into your bones. Then consider the widow who owns nothing but the ragged dress she wears on her shrinking frame.

She holds four hungry children close as she watches each of them starve to death. She has absolutely no source of income. She lives in a refugee camp. She's completely displaced with nothing to call her own. No address. No bills. No personal belongings. That one woman represents millions of women. As you recall the fear and strain of your financial woes, think of her. Ask God to intervene. Give to the poor. Pray for the displaced. *If you help the poor, you are lending to the Lord—and he will repay you!* (Proverbs 19:17).

Let's allow the energy of our experiences to make us mighty prayer warriors for those whose suffering we know and understand in part.

Each of us must find out what our work is to be and *what souls are entrusted to our prayers.* Let us make our intercession for them our life of fellowship with God, and we shall not only find the promises of power in prayer made true for us, but we shall also begin to realize how our abiding in Christ and His abiding in us allows us to share in His joy and blessing to the saving of souls[2] (emphasis mine).

—Andrew Murray

Years ago a friend candidly told me, "I don't understand apathetic Christians. With all of the suffering in the world, how can they be so self-indulgent as to be bored? Right now God has called me to the ministry of racial reconciliation, but if I didn't care so deeply about this issue, I'd work with the poor in the inner city and with the local food pantries. And if I weren't doing that, I'd likely work with a pro-life ministry for the sake of the unborn. And if not with the unborn, then I'd work with teenage girls who don't know who they are. As a believer in Christ, I've got a long list of causes and concerns that beckon my attention. My plate is quite full. I can't imagine being bored."

She makes a very strong point, but a great one. This is our day. This is our watch.

Anyone passionate about God and her faith will tell you that at some point God confronted her small thinking and selfish lifestyle. I'm there now (and I have a long way to go). Each new day I walk with God, my burden for those suffering increases. But this burden doesn't crush me; instead it fuels my resolve to make my life count. When I move toward those whom the world discards, I see God there. He is acquainted with the suffering soul. That's why He came.

> Speak up for those who cannot speak for themselves, for the rights of all who are destitute. Speak up and judge fairly; defend the rights of the poor and needy.
> (PROVERBS 31:8–9 NIV)

We who live in industrialized nations must constantly battle the currents of ambition, selfishness, pride, self-indulgence, apathy, inoculation from pain, and desensitization to sin. We must fight against the gods of comfort, materialism, and excess, and the idea that someone else's pain is not our problem.

Evangelist Billy Graham wrote, "We are slaves to our gadgets, puppets of our power, and prisoners to our security. The theme of our generation is: 'Get more, know more, and do more' instead of 'Pray more, be more, serve more.'"[3]

Jesus, the One we follow, was thoroughly acquainted with suffering, and not accidentally so. He intentionally headed to the slums where the lepers, the poor, and the oppressed lived. He was merciful to sinners and tough on the proud. He lived, breathed, and modeled Kingdom work so we might have His example to follow. Jesus heard the cries of the suffering; may we hear them too. He met their needs; may we follow His lead. He prayed for the sick, the wounded, the broken, and the demon possessed; may we pray as passionately as He. May the Lord Himself enlarge our capacity for courage, conviction, and compassion!

For he has not ignored or belittled the suffering of the needy. He has not turned his back on them, but has listened to their cries for help. (Psalm 22:24)

Is the prize not worth the price? Will you give up all to follow Jesus in the path He opens up to you? Will you fast when you feel it is necessary? Will you refrain from anything that hinders you in your life work—that of communing with God in prayer that you might become a person of faith whom He can use in His work of saving the world?[4]

—Andrew Murray

 ***Compassionate Lord,***

Make me more like You. I'm painfully aware of my sins and I ask for mercy, grace, and a renewed perspective. I can't carry my burdens, let alone those of the world. And yet You say that Your yoke is easy and Your burden is light. Show me what that looks like, Lord. Help me to live out my divine calling in such a way that my compassion and my convictions reflect Your heart mightily at work within me. One step at a time, sweet Jesus, I will follow You.

And now, Lord, I consider those who are desperately suffering at this very moment. Holy Spirit, pour out comfort and healing and restoration! Raise up a multitude of godly people willing to embrace the sufferings of others. Let us all be conduits of Your healing power. Release financial provision for those who have nothing. Move our hearts, shape our passions, and give us courage to be Your hands and feet for the least of these. Yes, Lord. Amen.

1. Read Psalm 82:3–4 and consider some tangible ways you can carry out these instructions. We can pray; we can send money to reputable organizations; we can read books on the issues and spread the word; we can organize a bake sale and raise money for a cause. There are a thousand things you and I can do to take a step toward justice. Pick one and carry it through.

2. Read Psalm 11:7 and rewrite this verse in your words.
   • Read Psalm 11:1–6 and take note of God's strong feelings toward those who are wicked and unjust. This is not a gray area for Him.

3. Read Isaiah 58:6–7 and consider this: God values obedience over sacrifice (see 1 Samuel 15:22). Yet the deeper we grow in Christ, the more often obedience is connected to sacrifice. These verses in Isaiah confront our comfort level. God doesn't want our leftovers or our attempts to compensate for when we mess up (His mercy has covered that). What He does want is our attention to the needs around us. To grow up in Christ is to tend to the things He cares about. Write a prayerful response to God's words in these verses.

4. To keep a balanced perspective, we must remember that we're not here simply for others. God cares about *our* hopes, *our* dreams, *our* pain, and *our* suffering as well. Much is said in the New Testament about how suffering produces character and perseverance in our lives. Still, God cares about our restoration. Read Isaiah 58:5 and notice how closely linked our personal healing and restoration is linked with the healing and restoration of others. Write out a prayer asking God to meet your current needs.

5. Read Isaiah 58:9–11. Notice the connection between "her freedom and your freedom." Please note that we don't earn merit by tending to the poor and suffering; we're simply obeying our Father, who cares deeply about what's happening on earth. Read this excerpt from my Bible commentary and then write out a prayer asking God to make this word your reality:

The godly one is assured that whenever he calls, the Lord will answer, "Here I am." If [she] will eliminate oppression, stop pointing the finger in accusation or in scoffing, and cease from mudslinging and slander, if [she] will alleviate the human need, both spiritual and physical, then God promises that his night will turn to day. [She] will enjoy guidance, abundant supply of good things, health and strength, beauty and fruitfulness, and national restoration.[5]

"Once your eyes are open to see injustice, it is near impossible to ignore it. What to do about it? Now, that's the big question. I've learned to never doubt the power of prayer. Pray diligently."

—ROYA, INTERN, IJM CAMBODIA

8

WAITING FOR
GOD TO ACT

*Put your hope in the Lord. Travel steadily along his path. He
will honor you, giving you the land. You will see the wicked
destroyed.* —PSALM 37:34

---

*Even though you may wait on God for many years, there is a
day coming when God will change everything in a moment of
time! He may take seemingly forever to get around to it, but
once God moves, He can change everything in a day.*[1]

—BOB SORGE

The morning was glorious, but my soul felt unsettled. I sat
out on the deck with my morning cup of coffee, listening to the birds
sing and longing for their cheery spirit. But my heart ached for my
son Jordan. Months earlier he had suffered a serious back injury
while playing football. Jordan's herniated disc pressed on three sets
of nerves, causing him unremitting pain. Oh, how I longed for him
to be healed!

One physician asked me if Jordan had lost control of his bowels
yet. Thankfully he hadn't. But each day I watched Jordan battle
through his pain, pushing back his frustration and disappointment.
One day he'd be victorious, and another, not so much. His daily

struggle weighed heavily on my spirit. "Give me a fresh perspective, Lord," I prayed.

Then the patio door opened. Jordan stepped onto the deck and found his place right beside me. I grabbed his hand and said, "You don't have to do this, you know. You don't have to go this morning if you're not feeling well."

"I know," he replied. "But I want to. I really need to get going, so can we pray now?" I nodded and we bowed our heads. And just as he did every morning, Jordan prayed, "Lord, I thank You for my life. And I thank You for my miracle. Thank You for completely healing me."

A familiar lump crawled into my throat as I passionately asked God for Jordan's miracle. The boy next to me was so tender, so sweet; I wanted him healed! Once we finished praying, Jordan carefully stood up. He wore a body brace that limited his mobility so he slowly made his way out the door and left for weight training at school. On strength training days, he cautiously did a few seated bicep curls because they didn't put pressure on his back. On running days, he carefully spent a couple of minutes on the elliptical at the lowest level possible. Even that was difficult for this seventeen-year-old, once-agile athlete.

Several months prior to that morning on the deck, when we were in the beginning stages of Jordan's injury, we had no idea just what a battle it would be. We tried everything we knew short of surgery to deal with his pain: chiropractic care, physical therapy, epidural injection, and daily decompression therapy. Nothing worked.

One day a friend told me that her husband had been miraculously healed from the same type of back injury. Days later, another friend told me of someone who also had been miraculously healed from the same injury. This friend strongly encouraged me to believe God for a miracle. That night I marched downstairs and found Jordan sitting on the couch, staring at the television. His perspective had atrophied along with his muscles. He was losing hope and didn't know what to do.

I knelt down by the couch, grabbed his arm, and said, "Jordan, I have something important to tell you." I couldn't get the words out fast enough. I relayed the two stories of healing. Then I said, "Jordan, I think these stories are for you. Let's err on the side of faith. Are you with me? Let's believe God for a miracle. What do we have to lose? We can't please Him without faith and we have the perfect opportunity to exercise our faith amidst this painful situation. Let's thank God for your healing every day. What do you say?" He looked me square in the eyes and said, "I'm with you. Let's do it."

And so he did. Every morning before he left for school, Jordan sat beside me, held my hand, and thanked God for his miracle. Then he'd brace himself to go to strength training, only to return before I even finished my prayer time.

The days blurred together. Watching him struggle to get through each day was almost more than I could bear. When he wasn't around, I'd get on my knees and cry out to God for a miracle. I heard numerous stories of thirty-year-old men who had injured their backs in high-school football only to be in constant pain and on disability. You can imagine what those stories did for my perspective.

Where once his brothers bantered and wrestled with Jordan, now they couldn't touch him. Jordan didn't feel much like joking around with them anyway, although he tried to be funny at times, and he really was. Oh, how I love my son.

So there I sat on my deck, looking to Jesus for a fresh perspective. And I found it in my injured son who was unrelenting in his prayers and in his conviction to show up and do what little he could do.

That same night, my husband and I sat side by side on our bed, both working on our laptops, listening to the news in the background. All of the sudden Jordan burst through our bedroom door with an energy and excitement we hadn't seen for six months.

"Mom! Dad! Look!" Jordan said. Then he forcefully bent over and touched his toes. He twisted and jumped and then kicked his leg high in the air. I stood on the bed with my arms in the air and screamed, "Jordan, what are you doing? Dear Jesus! Oh, my goodness, look at you! What happened?"

Eager to compensate for six months of immobility, Jordan kept moving his arms and legs and hopping up and down on the tips of his toes. Tears welled up in his eyes as he smiled and said, "Mom and Dad, God healed me tonight. I'm completely healed."

I came off of the bed and went right to my knees, burying my face in my hands and weeping, "Oh, Jesus, thank You." Then I got up, wrapped my arms around Jordan, and we cried together. I'll never forget that moment.

Earlier that night, Jordan had attended youth group. A young student who had just returned from a mission trip gave a not-so-eloquent but life-changing testimony. In so many words he said, "Yeah, so, I didn't really believe that miracles still happened today, but I guess they do. 'Cuz there was this sick kid on the mission trip and when I prayed for him, well, he was healed. So, yeah, God does still heal today."

When Jordan heard this boy's story, his heart beat faster. He sensed God telling him, *That's the boy I want to pray for you. Ask him tonight.* The rest of the youth group service continued with worship, a message, and prayer time. Afterwards, the leaders prayed for the kids who came forward. But Jordan knew he needed to find the student who had just returned from the mission trip.

Jordan carefully pressed through hundreds of students and finally found him, described his injury, and asked, "Would you pray for my healing?" The student unassumingly shrugged his shoulders and said, "Sure, yeah, okay." Then he placed his hand on the small of Jordan's back and began to pray. Jordan's back heated up during the prayer, but he didn't know what was happening.

When the boy finished praying, Jordan thanked him and then made his way out to the parking lot. Suddenly he stopped in his tracks. He felt different! Jordan moved slightly. No pain. He twisted gently. No pain. He reached down and touched his knees. No pain! He touched his toes and when nothing hurt, he took off sprinting around the parking lot, running as fast as he could. Though Jordan's a reserved guy, he ran back into the church yelling, crying and telling anybody who would listen that he had received a miracle.

The next morning I was out on the deck, holding my cup of coffee and singing along with the birds. I was beside myself with joy. All I could pray was, "Thank You, thank You, Jesus. Thank You, Lord." I heard the sliding door open behind me and out came Jordan, dressed in his workout clothes. He sat beside me, held my hand, and prayed the same prayer he'd been praying for the last couple of months, "Dear Lord, I thank You for my life. And I thank You for my miracle. Thank You for completely healing me." This was the same prayer he'd been praying for weeks on end.

> Yet the Lord longs to be gracious to you; he rises to show you compassion. For the Lord is a God of justice. Blessed are all who wait for him!
> (ISAIAH 30:18 NIV)

Jordan got up and went to strength training. This day Jordan ran with the team. He sprinted up and down the bleachers and, amazingly, kept up with most of the players. And when his teammates—who were used to seeing him hobble through his days—saw him run and sweat and smile, they asked him what had happened. Jordan had a captive audience to tell about his miracle, and he did. "God healed me last night. I'm completely healed."

Millions of people around the world wait right now for a

breakthrough. Some wait on God, looking for Him to act, believing that He will. Others set their eyes on other sources, biding their time as they wait for that next big thing: that next job, next house, next raise, next relationship.

No doubt a waiting-room season takes its toll on just about everyone, especially those with misplaced hope. Even we who believe in the living God can find it difficult to wait for Him to intervene in ways that tangibly change our circumstances. At times God seems agonizingly uninterested in our timetables and things don't always turn out exactly as we think they should or hope they will.

Godly people get sick and die. I've had some very godly friends—women of great faith—die of cancer. In fact, my friend Peggy told me, "The Lord will take me home when He gets more glory from my death than He does from my life."

I don't understand why one person gets healed and another (despite active, faith-filled prayers) never gets better. My brain can't comprehend why this is so. I don't understand miracles, healings, or sudden breakthroughs, but I do know they happen from time to time. I still wait for my healing. I've struggled for years with daily chronic health issues. Although I don't understand why some wait six days for their breakthrough while others wait sixty years, I'm still going to ask God to break through. The Bible says ask, and keep asking. Believe, and keep believing. Trust, and keep trusting. As I read God's living Word and ponder my son's miracle, I know anything is possible with God.

Praise the Lord, O my soul; all my inmost being, praise his holy name. Praise the Lord, O my soul, and forget not all his benefits—who forgives all your sins and heals all your diseases, who redeems your life from the pit and crowns you with love and compassion, who satisfies your desires with good things so that your youth is renewed like the eagle's. (Psalm 103:1–5 NIV)

As long as I have breath in my lungs, I'll cry out to God, "Forgive my sins! Heal my diseases! Ransom my life from the pit, crown me with loving compassion, satisfy my desires with good things, and renew my youth like the eagle's!" And with that same passion I'll keep asking God to rescue, redeem, renew, and restore those who suffer at the hands of evil people and desperately need literal freedom.

Precious Father,

Thank You for being such a faithful God. Forgive me for growing weary in waiting. Forgive my tendency to grumble and doubt. Help me to embrace an otherworldly perspective in this life. I'm learning that waiting seasons are actually times to cultivate an even deeper relationship with You. Help me to know Your Word, to believe Your truths, and to trust that You are good. You love me and You will come through for me. I will stand on that truth. Thank You, Lord.

And now, Lord, I pray for the desperately oppressed slave. Oh, God, if anyone needs a right-now miraculous breakthrough, he or she does! Please, Lord, hear my cry and set these prisoners free! Release them from the hands of wicked men and set them in safe homes. Heal their wounds and restore their souls. Renew them in every way. In Jesus' name, I pray. Amen.

initiate your freedom

1. Read Psalm 18:1–19. Insert yourself into this declaration. Picture the very real battle over your soul, your land, and the abundant life God has promised you. Consider some of the wicked ways the Devil has come against you. Now imagine your breakthrough. Picture yourself doing a victory dance. You *are* the object of God's affection, you know.

2. Now read the passage from Psalm 18 but this time with the sex-trafficking victim in mind. Picture her in an underground dungeon, desperate for rescue from vile forms of torture, manipulation, and rape. Go through this passage again and make it a declaration on her behalf. Picture her deliverance. Imagine her smiling and healed. Pray that she might be free. Her vulnerability is great but God's love for her is real. May our prayers keep all of heaven busy on behalf of these precious souls!

3. Read *The Message* version of Psalm 62:1–2: *God, the one and only—I'll wait as long as he says. Everything I need comes from him, so why not? He's solid rock under my feet, breathing room for my soul, an impregnable castle: I'm set for life.*

   • Does the above passage describe your perspective? How assured are you that everything you need is found in Him? Be honest.

   • What types of issues come up for you when you're forced to wait longer than you'd like? Why do you suppose that is?

   • If you've said yes to Jesus, you *are* set for life. Do you believe that? Have you put your trust in lesser things? We all do, to some degree, without even realizing it. Write a prayer asking for forgiveness and declaring that your hope is in the living God!

4. Read Psalm 40:1–5 (this passage carried me through some of my most desperate times). If you've been rescued from dire circumstances, read this passage out loud with a thankful heart! Remember the ways God has come through for you! If you're still waiting for a breakthrough, read this passage out loud with a thankful heart! Give Him the precious sacrifice of a grateful heart. Your declaration will bless Him and strengthen you.

"Through my experience I have seen that the road to justice is narrow. But God is almighty and He provides light and a way to fight injustice. I think sometimes He wants us to be still and wait for Him."

—KAKADA, SOCIAL WORKER, IJM CAMBODIA

9

Rejecting Captivity's Comforts

The people refused to enter the pleasant land, for they wouldn't believe his promise to care for them. Instead, they grumbled in their tents and refused to obey the Lord.   —Psalm 106:24–25

All earthly delights are but "streams." But God is the ocean.[1]

—Jonathan Edwards

This morning I woke up to the news that my friend Wendy passed away. Last week she went into cardiac arrest and survived too long without oxygen, suffering extensive brain damage. A young woman in her thirties, with a husband and two young children, Wendy died too soon.

Years ago, Wendy and I taught aerobics together. Eventually I retired from teaching. When I started taking classes, I was thrilled to be a participant in Wendy's class. Being in the studio with her was definitely one of my happy places; Wendy was my favorite instructor. I'd ride the bike in the front row of her cycling class and we'd have a great time bantering back and forth. Wendy, an advanced-level instructor, moved the class along at an excellent pace. When we weren't gasping for air because of one of her insane drills, we were gasping from laughter over something silly she said.

Wendy had a Cindy Crawford–like beauty, a hilarious sense of humor, an instinctive sense of rhythm, and an innate ability to make a whole studio of participants feel as though they were her best friends. Sometimes after cycling class, she and I would hang out in the studio and work on some fun hip-hop combinations together. The next thing you know, we'd be leaning on the bikes, conversing about life and about God.

I absolutely loved my friend Wendy. God poured abundant gifts into this woman. Still I'm convinced that Wendy didn't fully understand how valuable she was. Wendy lit up a room when she walked in, but she, like many of us, still had land to possess, soul freedom she never fully enjoyed while on this earth. Though Wendy possessed more talent in her little finger than most of us do in our whole body, I know she never totally comprehended how deeply loved and divinely called she was.

Last week I held Wendy's hand in the ICU and told her how much I loved her. At that moment, my passion for freedom increased significantly. As I prayed for my beautiful friend, I also thought of you. I thought of me. And I thought of every woman I'd ever had the privilege of meeting. Wendy's untimely death fuels my burning desire to make every day count and to fulfill the purposes God sets before me.

Wendy was a beautiful, gifted person, and I'll miss her forever. But it's important to note that physical beauty and giftedness lead nowhere if our thinking is off. You can be plain and not-so-gifted yet still change the world if you take God at His Word. Externals don't determine our greatness; understanding God's greatness *within us* makes all the difference.

It is no longer I who live, but Christ lives in me. So I live in this earthly body by trusting in the Son of God, who loved me and gave himself for me. (Galatians 2:20)

I want every woman I meet to become more God-aware than self-aware. I want each one to know in the depths of her being *true freedom*. I want us to know the vastness of our calling. We are all beautiful creations designed by a loving Creator, and God beckons us to freedom. No experience, sin, mistake, misstep, offense, or weakness can keep us from all we are meant to be in Christ. Even when we will make mistakes or people hurt and offend us, freedom is available right here, right now, in the midst of the mess.

Yet true inner freedom hinges completely on our belief system. Our past doesn't determine our future, but what we tell ourselves about that past does. The Bible calls us to take our thoughts captive, but all too often our thoughts hold us captive. How we think about what we've done—and what's been done to us—either will lead us on the path *to freedom* or on the road *to destruction*.

What we believe in this life directly affects *how we live*. And what we do on earth directly correlates with how we will live in eternity. That's why freedom matters so much. And freedom is possible in every season, every scenario, and every situation.

Consider Joseph in the Old Testament. He suffered unbearably at his brothers' hands. They stripped him of his robe, shoved him into an old well (wells like this were often used as graves), and then decided to sell him into slavery. Throughout this painful, unpredictable journey, Joseph responded to betrayal honorably; it's amazing when you think about it. Wherever Joseph ended up, God's blessing followed. Even so, Joseph was falsely accused of rape and unjustly imprisoned. But Joseph had a promise written over his life. And his consistent faithfulness beckoned God's favor and attention, and almighty God blessed the work of Joseph's hands.

As an unjustly imprisoned man, Joseph could have become bitter . . . enraged, even. But instead he grew in stature and honor. One day Joseph interpreted a dream for a couple of the king's servants who also were imprisoned. When Joseph's interpretation proved true, he asked the one servant to remember him on the outside, because Joseph was, after all, innocent. The man gladly promised Joseph that he'd return the favor, but then he forgot about Joseph. Imagine getting your hopes up, thinking your release and vindication were imminent, only to be overlooked again.

But one day, Joseph's breakthrough came. In a moment's time he was ushered from a grimy prison to a royal palace. He went from rags to riches in a matter of hours. What seemed like an agonizingly long journey actually was God's detailed plan to prepare Joseph for his destiny. God had readied his heart, character, favor, and skill. In fact, though it appeared that his brothers had left Joseph behind, the Bible tells it another way:

> [God] sent a man on ahead: Joseph, sold as a slave. They put cruel chains on his ankles, an iron collar around his neck, until God's word came to the Pharaoh, and God confirmed his promise. God sent the king to release him. The Pharaoh set Joseph free; he appointed him master of his palace, put him in charge of all his business to personally instruct his princes and train his advisors in wisdom. (Psalm 105:17–22 MSG)

God saw the need in Egypt. He knew about Egypt's impending famine and sent ahead the man who—by the time he arrived— would be right for the job.

Do you know that Joseph was more fruitful as a slave than his brothers were as free men? They had their freedom but were not free. They were evil. Joseph was a slave and a prisoner, yet everything he touched prospered. Joseph's captivity prepared him while his brothers' freedom condemned them. What we believe determines how we live.

Under the circumstances (Joseph) should have been upset. But he was not "'under the circumstances"; he was above them and saw God's hand in them. His time in prison was "training time for reigning time." So things that were meant for evil turned out to be for good.[2]

You know the story: Joseph's new place of promise involved horizons that stretched in every direction. Eventually he was promoted to the highest position in the land, second only to the Pharaoh. Joseph's divine preparation and God-given wisdom saved a nation in a time of famine. Joseph eventually married and had children. He named his second son Ephraim, which means *God has made me fruitful in the land of my suffering.*

If in our captivity we believe in God's Word and His goodness, and if we refuse attitudes of entitlement and bitterness, then in a little while the Enemy will be pushed off our land. We'll look carefully for the place he once occupied, but *he will not be there.*

Moreover, *in that very place* of loss and defeat, we'll enjoy an abundance of peace. But it doesn't stop there. We—like Joseph—will be able to look back at our journey through the wasteland and say that all was not wasted; in fact, God made us fruitful *even there.*

History tells the stories of some literal slaves who were free in spirit despite their chains. Isn't it astounding that even in such deplorable conditions as a concentration camp, a refugee camp, or a rice mill, certain slaves were freer than their masters?

Yet millions of people are literally free yet completely bound. This struggle is not new or exclusive to modern-day suburbia; Psalm 106:24–25 says, *The people refused to enter the pleasant land, for they wouldn't believe his promise to care for them. Instead, they grumbled in their tents and refused to obey the Lord.*

Many Israelites longed to return to Egypt because the pain of their slavery seemed more comfortable than the discomfort of the unknown. The fight for freedom is definitely not comfortable, predictable, or easy. Taking on new territory requires faith to get there and faith to stay there. The Israelites refused to enter the land God had for them because they refused to believe He was faithful. So they sat on their rumps and grumbled and gossiped, refusing to obey the Lord. They refused to believe the promise and then complained because their lives held no promise!

And so it goes with us. We refuse to believe God will come through for us so we "stay in our tents and grumble." We long for more than we're experiencing, but our limitations, past mistakes, fears of the future, love of comfort, and self-awareness prevent us from stepping into the best God has for us. So we buy. We eat. We drink. We waste time. We embrace fear, anxiety, doubt, and worry.

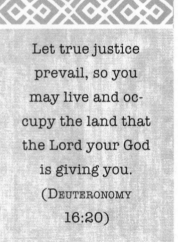

Let true justice prevail, so you may live and occupy the land that the Lord your God is giving you.

(DEUTERONOMY 16:20)

We cater to others' opinions. And we grab quick fixes, all the while missing out on the adventure of conquering new land.

We often feel the restraint of our shackles when we see other women moving toward freedom. We are tempted to envy or find fault with them. All the while God beckons *us* to be free! My friend Patty said it well: "You know that nagging feeling you have inside when you see others doing what deep down you want to do? It's meant to move you to pray, 'God, there's got to be more!'"

To that the Lord responds, "Oh, there is, My beloved one. You can't even imagine what a beautiful story I've written for you. Trust Me, and press on to be free."

Why *are* we so willing to stay captive than to accept the freedom offered to us? Blessed with living in a developed nation, we have so many comforts to prop us up. We never really *have* to feel the depths of our captivity if we don't want to. And if we never feel the depths of our soul confinement, we never become desperate for freedom or develop the tenacity to endure. We inoculate ourselves from the very pain that would provoke us to run for freedom!

You've heard it a thousand times, but it's still true: God isn't concerned with our comfort if it keeps us captive. He wants us free. He wants us to be brave and strong and true. He wants us to be full of holy ambition to pursue our next place of promise. And more new territory awaits you and me, dear sister.

Awesome God,

I want everything You have for me! Let it rain! Pour out Your Spirit on me and make me whole! Show me the places in my soul that sit in darkness and unbelief. Forgive me for embracing comfort and captivity over faith and freedom! Release in me a new tenacity to take hold of all You've taken hold of for me. Help me to know, on a deeper level, how loved and provided for I am. Don't let me live a lie, Lord! Help me to walk and live and breathe in the awesome light of Your truth.

And now, Lord, hear my prayer for my brothers and sisters in captivity. They are not comfortable! They are desperate for freedom. Hear our prayers and set them free! Expose the wicked ones who plot evil against the vulnerable. Shine a light on their dark meetings and bring them to justice. Open the prison doors for all who are unjustly held in captivity and set them completely free. Bring freedom to everyone in captivity! Thank You, Lord. Amen.

1. Read Psalm 116:10 and answer this question: What have you "believed and therefore said . . ." that is contrary to God's best for you? In other words, what have you told yourself about your circumstance that only creates within you more unbelief?
    - Turn that belief around. Rewrite a faith statement regarding your situation—one that ignites hope.

2. Read Psalm 116:16 and rewrite this verse inserting your situation. Declare that you belong to God. Thank Him for setting you free even if you don't *feel* free yet.

3. Before reading the next passage, think about the human-trafficking victim who sleeps on a filthy mattress on the floor. She is sure there is no hope for her; that no one knows she's there or cares that she's missing. Now read Psalm 142:4–7 and pray for her as you've never prayed before. Imagine throwing a freedom party for her!

4. Read Genesis 41:51 and write down the meaning behind the name of Joseph's firstborn son.
    - Read verse 52 and note the meaning behind the name of Joseph's second son.
    - Looking back at the painful places of your journey, what do you suppose God wants to help you forget?
    - In what ways has He made you fruitful amidst painful times?

5. Read 2 Timothy 2:9–12. Do you feel chained to circumstances beyond your control? If so, declare with the apostle Paul, "I may be bound, but God's Word is not bound! God's Word is free and powerful and working in and around me!" Look at the rest of the passage and remember this: when we suffer with Him, we also reign with Him. You're not subject to your captivity; you're a victor in spite of it!

6. Read John 8:36 and answer this question: In what ways has Jesus set you free?
    - Are you freer now than you were a year ago?
    - Envision your next place of freedom. How much freer would you like to be next year than you are today? Write a prayer asking your Good Shepherd to lead the way.

"Be aware of what's happening around you. So many times as Christians we tend to get in a bubble, just doing all the 'right things.' But then we just shut our eyes to everything else happening in the world. One step can make a change. It can be something very, very small. I think that's what we are here for."

—Madhu, assistant, IJM South Asia

Finding Refuge in God's Promises

The Lord is my rock, my fortress, and my savior; my God is my rock, in whom I find protection. He is my shield, the power that saves me, and my place of safety. —Psalm 18:2

He who is the God of the great world around us is the God of the little world within. It is He who is contending in thee; thou art but His soldier, guided by His wisdom, strengthened by His might, shielded by His love. Keep thy will united to the will of God, and final defeat is impossible; for He is invincible.[1]

—George Body

Several years ago I went with a group of women on a mission trip to Belize. We stayed in a small village, played with the children, did life with the families, and put together a conference for the women in the area. This trip, as did the other international ones I've taken, pushed me way out of my comfort zone. Nothing about that trip was easy for me. Almost every moment of the day, I felt unsure of myself and utterly aware of my fears. But God had me there for a purpose. In fact, as is often the case, I humbly received far more than I gave away.

While God lovingly protected us, many times things could have gone bad. One particular story of God's power, which cut through the very real spiritual oppression surrounding us, stands out. I've adapted this story from my book *Alone in Marriage: Encouragement for the Times When It's All Up to You.*

Nowhere else have I experienced such a tangible battle between the demonic and the heavenly—and the power available to those who belong to Jesus. I wrote this in my journal while I was there: *I'm in a place where I am quite sure that every single day angels and demons pass each other on the street.*

We were in a small, poverty-stricken village where dogs run wild and are often abused. These animals had a crazed look in their eyes and responded to the demonic activity level in the village by barking ferociously.

One day three friends and I walked to the church. We turned on a road we had taken many times before, but for some reason this time everything felt different. No moms were out doing their everyday chores and no children played. Instead several groups of scary, stoned-looking men glared and scowled at us.

Music played, drums beat in the background, and dogs ran all around in packs, barking at a feverish pitch. We felt a thick darkness pressing in and enveloping us; we could almost cut it with a knife. Suddenly we were outnumbered and felt isolated.

A couple of men narrowed their eyes and stepped toward us. They spoke in their native language, but by the tone of their voices and their facial expressions I knew they weren't telling us to "Have a nice day." My friend Ann grabbed my hand and I began to sing, "Jesus, what a wonder You are; You are so gentle, so pure and so kind; You shine like the morning star; Jesus what a wonder You are."[2]

Ann began to harmonize with me. We looked straight ahead, singing, walking, and refusing to be intimidated by the oppression around us.

Instantly, the presence of darkness was pushed back, making room for us to walk down an alleyway of light and peace. The dogs and the men stepped back a bit and continued to make noise, but their impact faded into the background. We kept singing and kept walking. Ann later described our worshipful prayer as a sword of light cutting through the darkness. For me, it was one of the most tangible expressions of God's power making way through the darkness that I have ever experienced.[3]

Many people came to know and trust in the Lord during World War II. One was an Englishman held in a German prison camp for a long period of time. One day he read Psalm 91. "Father in Heaven," he prayed, "I see all of these men dying around me, one after the other. Will I also die here? I am still young and I very much want to work in Your Kingdom here on earth." He received an answer, *Rely on what you have just read and go home!* Trusting in the Lord, he got up and walked into the corridor toward the gate. A guard called out, "Prisoner, where are you going?"

"I am under the protection of the Most High," he replied. The guard came to attention and let him pass, for Adolf Hitler was known as "the most high." He came to the gate where a group of guards stood. They commanded him to stop and asked where he was going. "I am under the protection of the Most High." All the guards stood at attention as he walked out of the gate. The English officer made his way

I will lead the blind by ways they have not known, along unfamiliar paths I will guide them; I will turn the darkness into light before them and make the rough places smooth. These are the things I will do; I will not forsake them. (Isaiah 42:16 NIV)

through the German countryside and eventually reached England, where he told how he made his escape. He was the only one to come out of that prison *alive*.[4]

A thousand may fall at your side, ten thousand at your right hand, but it will not come near you. (Psalm 91:7 NIV)

No doubt you have a few stories of God's intervention or protection. Still sometimes an arrow gets through or an imagined fear is realized. Then you wonder, *Where was God's protection? How come He allowed such a thing to happen?*

So how do we know if God's actually protecting us? After all, isn't God always with us? The Word says that we cannot get away from His presence. Everywhere we go, He is there (see Psalm 139).

The Lord sets wise boundaries for us because He knows how transient *we* are. When our sons were growing up, we made it clear to them that if they stayed within our guidelines, they would have a wonderful, provided-for, protected life. But should they stray beyond the lines we established for them, they could subject themselves to situations they were not yet equipped to handle, scenarios that could harm them, and consequences that could very well alter the course of their lives. We parented each son differently because we understood their weaknesses and strengths. Parenting our sons for adulthood required our involved, invested presence in their lives every step of the way. It's the same with us. But here's the difference: God never intends to relinquish His input. We need Him every hour.

We have an involved, invested heavenly Father. And because of our innate tendency to operate on autopilot, we need His continual influence as He directs us with the subtle shifts and changes required to keep us safe along the way.

God's arm is not too short to save us, but He's serious about how important it is for us to stay in step with Him. For example, God gave us a wonderfully wise precedent on giving. I've used this same concept for living. The Bible tells us to give cheerfully, not under compulsion or grudgingly (see 2 Corinthians 9:7). God doesn't want us tossing Him our leftovers and complaining the whole time. We are living sacrifices—holy and acceptable to God—ordained for a purpose! If we live or give reluctantly, everybody loses—mostly us.

I've used this same concept for living. God doesn't want us to live hastily, to give in to the emotion of the moment, because wise decisions are rarely made that way. He wants us to cheerfully *live*—with wisdom, preparation, and forethought.

> Live purposefully and worthily and accurately, not as the unwise and witless, but as wise (sensible, intelligent people), making the very most of the time [buying up each opportunity], because the days are evil. (Ephesians 5:15–16 AMP)

> Desire without knowledge is not good, and whoever makes haste with his feet misses his way. (Proverbs 19:2 ESV)

When we're serious about following Him, the Lord will lead us out of our comfort zone and fulfill His promise to love and protect us. Someone once said, "If He leads you to it, He'll lead you through it." Absolutely true. We can call on His many promises. We can trust Him to come through for us, and He will.

But to live "under compulsion" is to react to the moment or to drive ahead without a strong sense that God is leading the way. Maybe a conference or a trend or a passionate friend convinces you to take a giant risk that sounds like a good idea or is even for a good cause. But deep in your heart, there's no peace or personal nudge telling *you* to step out. Then don't. Because to do so would be to live under compulsion, which can get you into trouble.

Does it mean that God won't come through for you if you make a well-intentioned but unwise mistake? Not necessarily. However, I have heard one too many stories of disasters and near misses that could have been avoided had there been a higher priority on checking with God first. For our own good, He is so intent on teaching us to follow, to listen, and to obey that He'll let us burn our fingers if it keeps us from jumping into the fire without Him next time around.

> Righteousness and justice are the foundation of your throne; love and faithfulness go before you. (PSALM 89:14 NIV)

We're safest when we can stop when everyone else runs—if that's what God asks of us. We're safest when we're willing to jump, even when the crowd says it's impossible —if that's what God asks of us. We're safest when we're quick to listen and quick to obey. We're safest when we know God's promises and we hold them close to our heart. We're safest when we first and foremost identify ourselves as one who belongs to God and who is ever in His care. We make our plans and fight our battles and when the day is done, we rest in the shadow of His wings. What a privilege it is to be cherished and guided by the Most High God.

May we understand the seriousness of the call and the very real threat of dangers all about, but may our heart be strong and our eyes be fixed on Jesus. May we be wise enough to know when to hide in the shadow of His wings and when to shout a victory cry on the Rock of our Salvation! May we be valiant warriors who respect the Holy Spirit's guidance, knowing that He is our Comforter, our Protector, and the source of our divine Intelligence. May we be willing to take detours, to walk past enemies, and to go to foreign lands if that's what God asks. And may we know in the depths of our soul that the *center* of God's highest and best will is the safest place on earth. Yes, Lord.

Mighty Lord,

You are an awesome God, and I trust You. Help me to listen to Your voice and follow Your lead. I'm learning that self-protection makes for a small, ineffective life, while God-protection calls for expanded territories, faith-filled prayers, and fulfilled promises. That's the life I want. Lead me, protect me, and make my life count, Lord.

And now, Lord, I pray for every vulnerable young girl right now. Even if she doesn't know You, help her to hear Your voice. Don't let her be tricked into trusting the wrong people! Put a believer in her path where a perpetrator might have been. Cancel the schemes of the Enemy and establish the plans of the righteous. Protect every vulnerable soul today. In Jesus' name, I pray. Amen.

initiate your freedom

1. Read Psalm 91 every day for a month. Many soldiers embrace Psalm 91 as their promise of protection, and experience miraculous intervention as a result. Familiarize yourself with these promises.

2. Write down three significant times when God protected you (perhaps you were engaged in something careless, or you were faced with a very real danger and it eluded you).

3. Read Daniel 3:17–18 (if you're unfamiliar with the story, read the whole chapter). God reserves the right to be God. At some point in your faith journey, you must shift the weight of your belief onto God's faithfulness and determine that even if He doesn't come through for you as you wish, He's still God. Write a prayer declaring Him so.

4. Read Psalm 63:7–8. Spend time thanking Him for today's protection and guidance.

5. Read Psalm 5:11–12. Imagine yourself protected and favored by God. Write a prayer thanking Him for this promise.
   - Now write a prayer for your sister in captivity. Ask God to move heaven and earth to lead her to a place of safety.
   - Ask God to bring her to mind time and time again. Pray for her as often as the Lord brings her to mind.

6. When you're following *God's* lead, you can trust His protection. In what ways do you suppose God is asking you to step out next?

7. Read Psalm 73:23–28. If you feel so led, get down on your knees, open your hands, and surrender your life to the Lord. Embrace His promise of refuge. Give Him permission to lead.

"During every perpetrator investigation we talk to the perpetrators with [undercover] cameras; it's like going inside the lions' den. We do it only because of God's unconditional love—only His love and His power drive us to go and come back. With only me, I cannot do anything. It is my responsibility to show the same love to the people who are suffering."

—IJM INVESTIGATOR, SOUTH ASIA

11

DISARMING
THE PAST

*Not that I have already obtained all this, or have already been
made perfect, but I press on to take hold of that for which
Christ Jesus took hold of me . . . I do not consider myself yet
to have taken hold of it. But one thing I do: Forgetting what is
behind and straining toward what is ahead.*

—PHILIPPIANS 3:12–13 NIV

*Take your burdens, and troubles, and losses, and wrongs, if
come they must and will, as your opportunities, knowing that
God has girded you for greater things than these.*[1]

—HORACE BUSHNELL

After Mien was freed from forced prostitution through IJM
intervention, she began to heal in a safe and loving aftercare home
where she received an education, counseling, and vocational training. The perpetrators who trafficked her were convicted for their
crimes. Today, Mien lives with her family, works in a tailoring shop,
and *volunteers with children in the community center built in the very brothel
where she was first abused.* Everything has changed.

"My life changed from bad to good. In the past, I never had an
education. Now I go to classes. I am specializing in tailoring. It is
my dream to open a tailoring shop."[2]—Mien

I know a woman whose mother and brothers beat her as a child, yet she became an amazing mother to her children. I know another woman whose husband beat her, yet she opened a women's shelter for battered women. I know a woman whose husband was perpetually unfaithful, yet she still enjoys a pure and trusting relationship with her heavenly Father. And I know a woman whose childhood schoolmates relentlessly teased her, yet she became a youth pastor. Because of her passion, many young people today live for Jesus.

All of these women arose from the ashes of their past to live full, fruitful lives. They used the spoils of wisdom from their battles to secure freedom for others. And they continue to do so *today*. None of these women allowed their past to poison the present. Yet they refused to let those experiences go to waste. No, these women used their past pain as fuel for their present calling. The past serves them, not the other way around. My good friend Bonnie says it well, "I may be a product of my past, but I'm not a prisoner of it!"

Unfortunately, I've also known women who suffered minor offenses but refuse to let them go, women who have huge potential but a limited capacity for forgiveness or mercy. Past pains (both what happened to them and what happened through them) hold these women in bondage today. Their past still speaks, and they still listen.

The past—for all of us—must be reconciled if we ever intend to fulfill the God-sized call on our life.

So what does it mean to *disarm* our past?

Disarm: *To defuse, disable, deactivate, put out of action, make harmless*[3]

Okay, I have a bold question for you: Take the worst thing that's ever happened to you. Does it still hold you captive? I'm not asking if you returned to the state you were in prior to it. That can never be. You and I are different people because of our experiences.

Painful experiences change our perspective and even our approach to life. My husband was once a self-reliant man. Then he was diagnosed with cancer. Now he understands how fragile life can be. These days he begins every day confessing his utter dependence on God. Because of some scary things from my past, I'm more careful with my surroundings. Yet I'm passionate about squeezing every drop out of life after spending so many months in bed due to Lyme disease. My experiences have shaped me, just as Jesus, who rose from the grave with scars still in His hands, was deeply affected by what happened to Him down here.

Does the past still hold sway over *you*? Do you still overreact when faced with a situation reminiscent of that painful memory? My life still has areas that need healing. When I think of how broken I was, I never dreamed I would be as free —as whole—as I am now. But certain past memories still trigger present fears. Yet I am determined that with God's help, I will be free. I pray the same for you. So what about that trigger point? Do you have one?

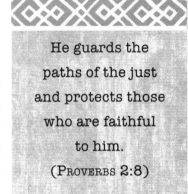

He guards the paths of the just and protects those who are faithful to him.

(PROVERBS 2:8)

Now picture the energy that surrounds your painful past being deactivated, disarmed, made harmless to affect your present. The scar is still visible, but there's no infection. You can look over your shoulder and acknowledge the experience happened, but it doesn't have the power to derail you; it doesn't get in the way of your ability to judge things clearly today. Ah, freedom. Here is a powerful truth: this kind of freedom is possible here on earth.

When I was a young girl, my identity and sense of safety were deeply affected by some things that happened to me at the hands of teenage boys. As a result, many years later my husband and I experienced a struggle in our intimate relationship. One day he gently said to me, "This isn't just my loss; it's yours too. The Enemy has stolen from both of us." God had been speaking the same thing to me. My husband's words lit a fire under me and compelled me to recover the lost territory that God (and my husband) longed for me to possess.

Years earlier, God taught me how to battle for lost ground when medical debts turned our finances upside down. We never seemed to get out of the hole we were in. More than anything, I wanted freedom in our finances; I wanted God's plan to prevail; I desired His path regardless of how uncomfortable or challenging it would be. With God's Word in our hearts, loads of prayer, and daily diligence, we recovered what financial territory we had lost and moved into a new land of promise. God delivered us! The Enemy's plan for our finances *fell apart.* Through one act of grace after another, God's plan for us broke through. The power of our painful financial past was disarmed. Amazing.

So to think that sexual intimacy was yet another area of freedom and blessing God had for me—well, that made me feel downright feisty! Instead of beautiful freedom and intimacy in lovemaking, I was stuck in a prison of frustration and misunderstanding, of past pain and condemnation. Once I realized I wasn't free, I was determined to become so.

It was time for me to step up and claim what was rightfully mine. Rightfully ours, that is. It was as though God had given us a king-sized bed and we were only sleeping on one corner of it. It was time to get my land (and our bed) back. Sorry about the pun.

I started to imagine the possibilities. What would it be like not to have to prepare mentally for intimacy? Wouldn't it be something to be completely free in my husband's arms? Where once our struggles weakened our unity, our lovemaking could actually strengthen us as a couple! For my husband's sake and mine, I had to get this land back!

The Devil camps on the assumption that we will live this life totally unaware of our God-given rights. The less we know about *who we are* and what we're missing, the more vulnerable we are to the Enemy's schemes.

When we were in Guatemala, an IJM lawyer told us, "The most vulnerable people in Guatemala are those who don't know or understand their rights as human beings. They are easy prey for those who would take advantage of them."

Our God is mighty and strong and true, and He is bent on our freedom and wholeness. Psalm 118:5 (NIV) reads, *In my anguish I cried to the Lord, and he* answered *by setting me free* (emphasis mine). We ask for a break, and He offers a *breakthrough.* We ask for relief and He offers us freedom. Jesus is not interested in making us more comfortable for the moment if it binds us to our past mistakes and wrong beliefs. He wants us free! He is intent on our freedom and He wants us to desire it as much as He does. Our faith requires us to say no to the Enemy, to draw a line in the sand. At some point—with the Lord at our side—we must learn how to battle.

Ask God to give you a fresh perspective on your level of freedom. If you've lost your identity, ask Him to help you recover it. Boldly ask the Lord for an appetite for freedom. May every cord that binds you be cut loose in Jesus' name! Declare out loud: "In Jesus' name, I disarm the power of my past and I leverage my experiences for a powerful, present-day calling. I will not allow my past to speak to me except to teach me! I reject the Enemy's plan to imprison me and I embrace God's beautiful plan of freedom for my life!"

For the believer, every new day is a chance to begin again. We are freshly forgiven, powerfully provided for.

When I consider the daily horror that slaves and trafficking victims endure, I'm amazed that *any* of these rescued victims pursue further education, get married, have children, and enjoy sunny days. Unfortunately, many more women and girls live and die in captivity than ever get rescued. But thanks to patient, godly aftercare workers, a good number of these precious souls who do escape experience healing. I'm inspired when I read stories of trafficking victims who become fruitful victors. Some of these brave girls actually assist undercover investigators to plan raids on brothels so more girls might be freed. Their courage both inspires and confronts me.

So how easy is it to disarm our past? For some it's like flipping on a light switch. One minute they believe a lie, the next they understand the truth. For others, extended times of prayer ministry or counseling are necessary.

Still, I've known folks who have undergone years of counseling yet never become free simply because they never confront the lie they believe. They overprocess their pain and their feelings about the pain, but they never actually address the source of their captivity.

Let's take a look at some practical ways we can initiate our freedom:

Identify the area of captivity. It wasn't too difficult for me to identify my area of captivity. I struggled in our intimacy and my husband paid a price for it. It's painful to be honest about our captive areas, but it's the first step to freedom.

Can you easily discern an area in which you're captive? If not, ask a trusted friend; she'll tell you. And definitely pray about it. Ask the Lord to reveal the ways you've made accommodations for your captivity. Ask Him to show you the path to freedom. A slave's captivity is obvious. It's harder for a literally free woman to nail down the boundaries of her captivity. Remember the recently rescued slave as you process this.

Identify the lie. Once you realize an area that God wants to set free, you must discern the lie that holds you captive. This lie is the Enemy's most powerful tool. But once you permit God to shine His light in your life, He will expose your wrong thinking and core beliefs. This painful process is necessary if you wish to truly be free.

Some identify a lie during a morning prayer time, and in a moment's time they are free. More often it takes a pastor, counselor, or other godly person who has walked through a similar experience to take you by the hand and help you face what is buried in your past. This is rarely easy but truly liberating.

I believed the lie that sex was a dirty thing. For the life of me, I couldn't figure out how to see it as beautiful in the context of marriage. When I finally admitted that I believed a lie, I confessed and repented of my white-knuckle grip on it and asked God to flood me with more of His truth.

Replace the lie with the truth. This is the fun part! For every lie you believe, God provides a corresponding truth. Once you pull out the weeds, you must plant some good seeds. Memorize Scripture promises that God gives you. Find passages that directly correlate to your situation. Guard your yard and cultivate the growth of your freshly planted seeds by daily spending time with Jesus.

Another way to reinforce the truth is to read great Christian books. I found several wonderful resources on how to embrace godly intimacy within the marriage. I found I was not alone. Freedom was at my fingertips.

Help secure the freedoms of others! Now is the time to leverage your experiences to help others discover the freedom you enjoy. Ask God to increase your sphere of influence; to show you whom He has entrusted to your care; and to awaken your compassion for those awaiting rescue, be it literal or spiritual. It is for freedom that Christ has set us free. Her freedom, your freedom, my freedom: God cares about all of these, and we need each other on this journey.

As much as I'd like to keep parts of my story private, I've seen firsthand how God uses my brokenness to bring healing and freedom to others. Self-preservation must go if we want to be the kind of vessel God can use for His glory!

God in heaven,

You are my Deliverer. By Your mighty power, disarm the power of my past! Take me by the hand and lead me to places of truth. Expose in me the lies that hold me captive. Liberate me from painful memories and wrong beliefs. I want to live a brave, free life, just as You did. Lead me in Your everlasting way. Thank You, Lord.

And Father, my mind cannot comprehend the pain and trauma so many have experienced at the hands of wicked men. But You understand, Lord. Hear my prayer and pour out Your healing power on every desperate soul! Bless the aftercare workers with patience and perspective. Fill their cups so they'll have what they need to do this important work. Bring freedom and victory where there was once captivity. Move in power, Lord. Amen.

1. Read Psalm 31:3–4 and describe one way the Enemy consistently uses your past to entrap you.

2. Read verse 3 again as a prayer. Write a prayer letting God know that you will trust Him to guide you.

3. Read Psalm 31:7–8 and take a risk here. First thank God that you are still standing! You *are* an overcomer! With regard to your painful past, describe the "anguish of your soul" that resulted from your experience.

   • Write down what you think is God's perspective on your experience. This might be difficult, but give it a try.

   • Look at verse 8 again and consider Mien returning to volunteer at a community center that stands where the brothel was.

   • Imagine what kind of spacious place God is preparing for you (e.g., victory where once was defeat; life where once was death). Write it down.

4. Read Psalm 103:4–5. Get excited about God's redeeming power. Call on Him to move on your behalf, because He will. Share your vision of freedom with someone today. This is an important part of freedom's journey.

5. Read Psalm 31:24 and do what it says. Put your hope in the Lord and then be strong and courageous. He is for you and He will deliver you.

> "Justice brings back what suffering and oppression
> have taken away: hope."
>
> —Pablo, field office director, IJM Guatemala

12

Refusing
to Blend In

His divine power has given us everything we need for life and godliness through our knowledge of him who called us by his own glory and goodness. Through these he has given us his very great and precious promises, so that through them you may participate in the divine nature and escape the corruption in the world caused by evil desires. —2 Peter 1:3–4 niv

If God were to remove from us the possibility of disobedience there would be no value in our obedience, it would be a mechanical business.[1] —Oswald Chambers

A number of years ago, I fell asleep with the television on. I'd been watching news on the war, so I must have had visions of soldiers running through my brain as I dozed off and began dreaming. At first my dream didn't seem significant, but over time, it has provided me with great insight. Unlike my other dreams, I wasn't actually in this one, but I watched it from above, as though I was in heaven looking down. From my vantage point, I could understand what those on the ground didn't. I couldn't say anything; I simply watched the story unfold.

In it, thousands of highly trained soldiers split into groups and were sent to different assignments. One particular battalion went deep into the jungle to set up camp and await their next assignment.

Once the soldiers arrived at their designated spot, they inventoried their supplies and set up camp for the night. They pulled out their weapons to keep a watch on their surroundings. Daily the soldiers mentally rehearsed their drills, reviewed their maps, and checked their equipment. They were ready to receive their next marching orders.

One day some children wandered into the camp. The soldiers looked around for their parents and when none were found, they fed the children and played games with them. It was a nice break. Later in the day, the children's mother found her way to the camp and retrieved them, but first stayed for a bit and chatted with the soldiers.

The next day several more villagers came to the soldiers' camp with gifts of baked goods in hand. Day after day the villagers and the soldiers crossed paths. They talked, shared meals, and became friends. Eventually the village women offered to wash the soldiers' uniforms. The soldiers spent more time in the village, eating the villagers' food, playing their games, and wearing their clothes. Without even realizing it, the soldiers slowly forgot about their post and their drills.

From an insider perspective, this battalion had the sweetest of assignments. The soldiers made great friends, ate delicious food, and enjoyed a leisurely life. Unfortunately, over time the soldiers stopped looking like soldiers and resembled the villagers. All the while, soldiers stationed in other locations daily battled the elements and faced their opponents. These soldiers remained sharp, fit, skillful, alert, and ready for whatever they were called to do.

One day the village-soldiers received their call to move to their next location. Intelligence informed the commanders that if these soldiers did not change their position, they would possibly be ambushed. When the soldiers didn't reply to their commander, an outside soldier was sent in to make sure they were all still alive, only to discover these AWOL soldiers were fat, happy, and completely out of shape.

The end of the dream was quite sobering. The soldiers were wiped out. And the kind villagers? They were a plant used by the other side to seduce the soldiers out of battle mode and into leisure mode, rendering them useless and ineffective.

> Freedom does not mean I am able to do whatever I want to do. That's the worst kind of bondage. Freedom means I have been set free to become all that God wants me to be, to achieve all that God wants me to achieve, and to enjoy all that God wants me to enjoy.[2]
>
> —Warren Wiersbe

> Soldiers don't get tied up in the affairs of civilian life, for then they cannot please the officer who enlisted them. (2 Timothy 2:4)

Whether we believe it or not, we *are* divinely created and divinely called. Our Maker deserves our honor and affection. He is profoundly worthy of our complete surrender so that He might do His greatest work in and through us. His highest will for us is our best-case scenario.

Yet we live in a world full of distractions, indulgences, and lesser gods. And so here lies the test: Will we go our way and feast on this world's stuff or will we embrace Christ's refining call and honor the One who entrusted this life to us?

Obviously we're not called to live in a Christian bubble, totally removed from a lost and dying world. In fact the Bible states we're to be *in* the world but not *of* it. Jesus came for the lost and the least and to set us free. This is our call as well. But if we share the world's addictions, sinful tendencies, and same worries and fears, what does that tell the lost about our saving God? Our lack of freedom speaks a message, and Christ's gospel of redemption gets lost in translation.

A couple of years ago I read a George Barna report that stated very few distinguishable differences exist between Christians and non-Christians today. We've blended with the masses to the point that we've lost our voice and influence. For the sake of these desperate times and of those in literal shackles, we must rise to our rightful place as ones who honor the living God. When we take the call on our life seriously, God takes the prayers that come out of our mouth seriously!

When one soul says a resounding yes to God's plan for her life, a supernatural shift in both the physical and the spiritual realms occurs. Things change all around us when we choose radical obedience instead of selfish indulgence.

As we step into the things of God and obey His Word, our life will be marked by power. And that's the stuff of the Kingdom.

> For the message of the cross is foolishness to those who are perishing, but to us who are being saved it is the power of God. (1 Corinthians 1:18 NIV)

In the Old Testament, Abraham and Lot provide a great contrast of what it means to honor God and to blend with godless people. Spend some time reading Genesis; notice how often Abraham called on the Lord's name and how often the Lord blessed Abraham. In fact, as believers, we inherit Abraham's blessing (see Galatians 3:9).

Since the land couldn't sustain both Abraham and his nephew Lot, Abraham knew they needed to part ways. Abraham gave Lot the choice of the land, and Lot grabbed what he thought was the most prime property. In time, Lot realized that he had pitched his tent among some exceedingly wicked men, yet he stayed there. His conviction didn't compel him to move!

Although Abraham had temporary lapses in judgment, he honored God. And God, in return, honored Abraham. God's amazing willingness to listen to those who love Him is revealed through an exchange He had with Abraham. God wanted to destroy Sodom (the place where Lot lived) because of its wickedness, yet He listened to Abraham's plea to spare the righteous who still lived there. Back and forth they went: "Will you destroy Sodom if you find fifty righteous in the land? . . . How about forty-five? . . . Thirty? . . . Twenty?. . . Ten?" (see Genesis 18). The Lord honored Abraham's request. What an incredible privilege it is to have the listening ear of almighty God.

Maybe you know the story. In answer to Abraham's prayer, a couple of angels went to Sodom to rescue Lot from the town's iminent destruction. But Lot still had some decisions to make. While the angels were inside Lot's home, all of the men from every part of the city, both young and old, pounded on the door and demanded to have sexual relations with the visitors. It's hard to imagine such depravity.

In Middle Eastern culture, guests were treated with great honor and given the best a host had to offer. When you consider the generous hospitality that marked the culture of Lot's day, it's painfully clear that the moral decline of Sodom was more than appalling.

In an effort to spare his guests, Lot offered to toss his two virgin daughters out to the angry mob. Unbelievable, really. Because of its blatant dishonor of God, this town was on the brink of destruction. Just as my dream's village-soldiers lost their edge when they needed it most, Lot lost his sense of identity, of calling, of moral clarity when he needed it most. These things don't happen overnight.

Second Peter chapter 2 records Lot as a righteous man who became distressed by the immorality around him. Unfortunately, by living among such evil men, Lot lost some major spiritual ground.

As a result, in a time of great moral crisis his words meant nothing. Let's look at the effectiveness of Lot's plea to his future sons-in-law: *So Lot went out and spoke to his sons-in-law, who were pledged to marry his daughters. He said, "Hurry and get out of this place, because the Lord is about to destroy the city!" But his sons-in-law thought he was joking* (Genesis 19:14 NIV).

William Penn, the founder of the province of Pennsylvania, was a strong defender of democracy and religious freedom. He wrote this: "Those who will not be governed by God, will be ruled by tyrants."[3]

The ripple effect of Lot's choice to blend with godless people is staggering. Thanks to Abraham's intercession, Lot escaped Sodom with his daughters but not his wife. Despite the chaotic confrontation and her daughters' potential rape, Lot's wife still wasn't ready to leave town. She looked back and lost her life. This kind of desensitization to sin doesn't happen overnight.

One night, in a dark cave, Lot's daughters got him drunk and slept with him. They each got pregnant by their father. Lot's daughters were products of their environment. Their situation reminds me once again of the importance of embracing our God-given call. Every life counts because of the value and destiny attached to it. If we live for the Lord, the ripple effect goes on for generations. If we go our own way, the ripple effect goes on for generations. There's so much at stake. Lot had a couple of children with his children. Read this excerpt from my *Believer's Bible Commentary*:

> The older daughter subsequently bore a son named Moab, and the younger bore a son, Ben-Ammi. Thus began the Moabites and the Ammonites, who became recurring thorns in Israel's side. It was the Moabite women who later seduced the men of Israel to commit immorality (Numbers 25:1–3) and the Ammonites who taught Israel the worship of Molech, including the sacrifice of children (1 Kings 11:33;

Jeremiah 32:35). We know from 2 Peter 2:7–8 that Lot was a just man, but because of his worldliness he lost his testimony.[4]

Facing a raging sex-crazed crowd outside our door seems far removed from us, but the sins of Sodom are right in our midst: *Sodom's sins were pride, gluttony, and laziness, while the poor and needy suffered outside her door* (Ezekiel 16:49).

Our culture is inundated by sexual images and perversion. We are surrounded by overdoses of self-importance; we squander hours on media, consumerism, and materialism. We consume countless meals where we eat way past fullness. These things make us soft, weak, and ineffective. When we make self-indulgence a lifestyle, we fall into the same trap as the soldiers in my dream.

We work to feed our appetites; meanwhile our souls go hungry (Ecclesiastes 6:7 MSG). Meanwhile the poor, the slave, and the oppressed suffer right outside our door. And this is a very big deal to God.

> The nation of Israel is the vineyard of the Lord of heaven's armies. The people of Judah are his pleasant garden. He expected a crop of justice, but instead he found oppression. He expected to find righteousness, but instead he heard cries of violence.
> (ISAIAH 5:7)

"For I was hungry, and you didn't feed me. I was thirsty, and you didn't give me a drink. I was a stranger, and you didn't invite me into your home. I was naked, and you didn't give me clothing. I was sick and in prison, and you didn't visit me." Then they will reply, "Lord, when did we ever see you hungry or thirsty or a stranger or naked or sick or in prison, and not help you?" And he will answer, "I tell you the truth, when you refused to help the least of these my brothers and sisters, you were refusing to help me." (Matthew 25:42–45)

Blending in is only good if you're in the choir or in a bad part of town. God offers believers so much more than the muddy water and the entanglements of this world. We're given the opportunity to participate in God's divine nature. He offers His peace, His power, and His promises to those of us whose hearts are fully devoted to Him. When we take Him at His Word, His Word will work powerfully through us.

But we are only as strong as our weakest link. And unfortunately, at least according to statistics, far too many believers live double lives. This has nothing to do with adhering to a legalistic list of dos and don'ts. On the contrary, true freedom is being free from the things that steal life and land from the masses, be they addictions to food, drink, approval, money, or stuff. True freedom starts with knowing God's love is *better* than life. Living for Him is the soul's greatest honor.

When our boys were young, we wanted to teach them about the importance of personal holiness and how that affects the entire Christian community. We stood in a circle, held hands, and talked about the incredible value God places on each of our lives. Then I said to my sons, "You are gatekeepers. What you allow in your lives, you allow in ours. You have a very important role in this family. Guard your heart and watch your gate, for the sake of your life and for the strength of this family."

The body becomes stronger as its members become healthier. The whole church of God gains when the members that compose it begin to seek a better and higher life.[5]

—A. W. Tozer

 ***Holy God,***

Forgive me for the countless ways I have blended with a godless people. Forgive me for allowing my senses to be dulled and my convictions to be curbed. I want more of You, Lord. Fill me afresh with Your Holy Spirit and create in me a clean heart, O God! Restore to me the joy of Your salvation and renew a right spirit within me. I want Your highest and best will for me. Lead me in Your everlasting way.

And now, Lord, I pray for the millions of girls who blend in with a sex-crazed society but so desperately want to be free. Set them free, Lord! Hear my prayer and heal the deepest places in their souls. Bring a fresh purity and hope to their hearts. Set them on a path of complete restoration. Surround them with people who love them. In Jesus' name, I pray. Amen.

initiate your freedom

1. Read Luke 17:26–33. It's sobering to think that it'll be business as usual up to the end. Are you more attached to your life on this earth, or your life in Christ? Be honest. Ask the Lord to show you what He'd like you to surrender to Him.

2. Read Matthew 25:1–13. Rewrite this scene with a modern-day setting.
   • Why do you suppose the virgins without the oil didn't feel the need to be prepared?
   • How would you apply verse 13 to your life?

3. Read Jeremiah 2:11–13. Isn't it amazing how true these verses stand even today? What are some of the gods of this age?
   • Imagine the heavens gasping when you and I choose a quick fix rather than go to the Lord with our need. If one comes to mind, spend a moment asking God's forgiveness.
   • According to verse 13, what two evil sins were committed? So it goes today. Write a prayer asking God's forgiveness on behalf of your nation.

4. Read Hebrews 12:1. Imagine the cloud of witnesses cheering you on— because they are! Ask God to help you remember that you are never alone. Greater are those who are for you than those who are against you.
   • What weights slow you down? Bring these before the Lord. Ask Him for grace to make a change.
   • What is the sin that so easily entangles you? How often are you exposed to this sin? What steps can you take to protect yourself?

5. Read Galatians 2:20 and write out a statement declaring your redeemed life in Christ.

"What would Jesus do in the face of an evil like human trafficking? The Jesus I know would condemn those who exploit the weak and show mercy to girls trapped in the sex trade. As Christians we need to be the miracle that we're praying for God to send—the Church should be taking the lead and doing what Christ would do."

—RICHARD, COMMUNITY MOBILIZATION OFFICER,
IJM SOUTH ASIA

Trusting God to Be Big in Us

CLAIRE'S* STORY

Don't be afraid, for I am with you. Don't be discouraged, for I am your God. I will strengthen you and help you. I will hold you up with my victorious right hand. —ISAIAH 41:10

God has set a Savior against sin, a heaven against hell, light against darkness, good against evil, and the breadth and length and depth and height of grace that is in himself for my good, against all the power and strength and subtlety of every enemy. [1]
—JOHN BUNYAN

When Claire's* husband passed away, she struggled to care for their four young children while dealing with serious chronic health issues. As were most of her neighbors, Claire was poor, but she built a life for her son and three daughters in the small home she and her husband had shared outside of Uganda's capital city, Kampala.

Nearly five years after her husband's death, a foreign investor purchased a nearby plot of land, and Claire's very modest house increased in value. When her late husband's relatives learned of the development, they came to Claire's home for a family meeting and made a shocking announcement: They were kicking Claire and her children out of her home, selling it, and keeping the profits—and there was nothing she could do to stop them.

*Not her real name. Claire's story courtesy © International Justice Mission

Though a woman's right to shared property in a marriage is guaranteed by Ugandan law, a widow is often at the mercy of her deceased spouse's relatives, who use her vulnerability to lay claim to any property that belonged to the couple. Property grabbing from these most defenseless members of a community leaves widows and orphans with nowhere to live, nowhere to work, and nowhere to grow food. This theft is not just a matter of property, it's a matter of survival.

Panicked, Claire reported her relatives' threat to local authorities, but the perpetrators distorted the truth. Claire was left without an ally. She tried to work out a temporary agreement with her relatives to stop them, but they moved forward with their illegal plan and met with a potential buyer. Despite the fact that the relatives had no proof of home ownership, the buyer readily agreed to the deal.

The day before the sale was to go through, Claire discovered what was about to happen. She was terrified that she and her four young children were about to become homeless.

Throwing Claire out of her home was a death sentence. She did not have the resources to purchase another house for her family. The only place she would be welcome was her home village in a remote district—far from the hospital care she needed to manage her illness. Without this care, she would die.

Claire learned about IJM from a counselor in her community and immediately called the Uganda office. An IJM attorney quickly called the interested buyer and warned him that the purchase was illegal. The call was placed just in time: the buyer agreed to delay the sale.

Though Claire was safe from immediate danger, she needed long-term legal protection. So IJM's staff arranged for legal mediation to establish Claire's right to her property.

One balmy morning, Claire, her relatives, the interested buyer, and IJM attorney Juliet Musoke gathered for a legal meeting of life-

and-death importance. While the proceedings took place in Claire's modest brick house rather than a grand marble courtroom, she courageously stood up to the perpetrators. With a strong advocate on her side, Claire was not alone.

Juliet explained to the perpetrators that their actions were illegal and indefensible—and that she was willing to take them to the highest court in the land to ensure that Claire and her children were not left destitute and homeless.

The perpetrators lost their swagger. When they realized that Claire would not be bullied into homelessness, her relatives dropped their claim.

Juliet drew up a legally binding document for all present to sign, stipulating Claire as the sole owner of the property. The message was clear: Claire was not alone; she was not disposable. The law—and strong advocates—were on her side. Her response was simple: "I am overjoyed," she told IJM staff.

Today Claire is safe. She and her family live with hope for a secure future. IJM aftercare staff assist her in her pig-raising business, a sustainable income source for her children and her.

When IJM Uganda launched an intensive program in Claire's community to protect widows' property rights, they asked her to speak to the audience. Before a crowd of nearly one hundred people, including local government officials, press members, and church leaders, Claire shared with grace and confidence the truth: she and her children can now live in peace.

Wait passionately for God, don't leave the path. He'll give you your place in the sun while you watch the wicked lose it. (Psalm 37:34 MSG)

 **Precious Lord,**

You are my great Defender, and I can trust in You. Just as IJM stepped in on behalf of Claire, You will stand in the gap for me. You will help me recover the land the Enemy has stolen from me. Help me not to lose hope or grow faint in the battle. In due time, the Enemy will lose his grip on what rightfully belongs to me. Victory is mine because I am Yours. Thank You, Jesus.

And now, Lord, I pray for Claire and every precious widow she represents. Be her great Defender and Protector. Provide for her needs and strengthen her relationships. Multiply her food, increase her faith, and renew her perspective. Keep her close to Your heartbeat and her enemies far from her. In Jesus' name, I pray. Amen.

No study questions today

Taking Every
Thought Captive

*We demolish arguments and every pretension that sets itself up
against the knowledge of God, and we take captive every
thought to make it obedient to Christ.* —2 Corinthians 10:5 niv

*If a man leaves his garden alone, it very soon ceases to be a
garden; and if a saint lets his mind alone, it will soon become
a rubbish heap for Satan to make use of.*[1]

—Oswald Chambers

During the wintertime, we keep the temperature in our
house at about sixty-seven degrees—way too cold for the dog and
me. Good ole Bubs moves around the house to camp on the floor by
the window that reflects the most sun at the moment. If I didn't
have so much to accomplish in a day, I'd join him.

Minnesota winters are brutal. We warm up our cars to drive a
mile down the street. We go to bed with layers on. We cook warm
meals and then prop open the oven to warm the house. And we like
to snuggle.

Every once in a while, when Kevin and I feel a cold draft blow-
ing through the house, we wonder if there's a door open somewhere.
But we don't stop there. We go on a hunt to find how that frigid
draft got in.

When we experience that bone-chilling draft, we know one of us (probably one of our sons) left a door cracked open. When there's a twenty-below wind chill outside, you feel as though you're outside even when you're in! Besides, it's a waste of energy *not* to keep your home sealed tight in the winter. My dad repeatedly said, "I don't have enough money to feed all seven kids *and* heat the outside. Make sure the door is shut!"

Maybe you live in a place that stays toasty all year round. I'll try not to be jealous. But for the sake of illustration, imagine that your house represents your mind. Imagine that the heat that warms your home is God's transforming Word. The open doors and windows are the thoughts that expose you to the elements outside (and allow God's Word to escape).

In order to enjoy a healthy mind-set, we must, as Oswald Chambers stated, faithfully *cultivate and then maintain* a redeemed thought life. Our thought patterns require constant attention, and if we neglect such work, our life will be marked by defeat, captivity, and inconsistency. Furthermore, it's quite possible to be free in one area of thinking and captive in another.

Some people grow beautiful flower beds in their front yard (the part that everyone sees), and weeds and thickets in the back. Some people function well in the workplace, but are completely dysfunctional in relationships. Some women are phenomenal mothers yet care nothing for themselves, their health, or their spiritual life. Others exercise their body and their mind but are completely selfish with their time. Some women are perpetual servants but cannot bring themselves to receive a gift or a compliment. We all have undeveloped places on our land.

God intends for Christ's resurrection power to swallow up death—in every area of life. He wants every nook and cranny of our land to be healthy, beautiful, thriving, and weed free.

In order to fully embrace our freedom, we need to look at our thought processes and identify the open doors that leave us vulnerable. These are the places where our thinking is off, where God's Word escapes us, and where deceptive thoughts squeeze in.

One day many years ago, I asked God to heal me from some chronic health issues. His response that particular day surprised me:

I could heal you today, but you'd lose it tomorrow. Your mind-set does not support healing right now. Your thoughts are more consumed with sickness than they are with well-being and health. Start thinking healthy thoughts. Start trusting in My Word more than your feelings. Take captive your wandering thoughts and make them obedient to Me. When you get to a point where you're consistently thinking like a healthy person, you'll be positioned to walk in complete health. You've succeeded at imagining the worst. Now it's time to imagine the best, hope for the best, and believe for the best.

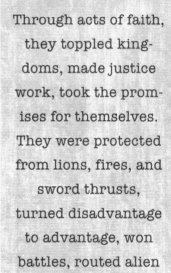

Through acts of faith, they toppled kingdoms, made justice work, took the promises for themselves. They were protected from lions, fires, and sword thrusts, turned disadvantage to advantage, won battles, routed alien armies. (HEBREWS 11:33–34 MSG)

This insight knocked me over! I realized the lines between my actual health battles and my fears had completely blurred. My thoughts were consumed by my symptoms, my fears, and my limitations. It didn't matter that I regularly spent hours in God's Word. All of my doors and windows were open to the elements outside!

I had spent so many years battling Lyme disease, tending to sick babies in the hospital, and watching my husband fight cancer that I couldn't get past the constant fear of debilitating health issues. Yet as soon as I applied God's instruction to my thought patterns, I felt stronger. I was stronger. But it took regular, grueling practice to think more on the Lord's strength than on my weakness.

> I pray that out of his glorious riches he may strengthen you with power through his Spirit in your inner being. (Ephesians 3:16 NIV)

Granted, even today I deal with some major digestive issues and a few other health struggles that get in my way. But I think and behave as though I were completely healthy. And except for those few times when I experience a flare-up, I *feel* healthy. Those who don't know that I struggle would never guess that I do. I guess that's the point; I don't struggle anymore. I stand on God's Word. I endure the occasional flare-up with trust, belief, and surrender. But all in all, I am now superhealthy; one day I believe I'll enjoy complete healing!

Developing this mind-set isn't about concentrating on the object of your desire, unless, of course, that desire is Christ Himself. It's preparing a way for the Lord, making a straight path for Him (see Matthew 3:3). This Scripture refers to any sin that hinders the Lord from having *His complete and perfect way* in our life.

The extent to which we strengthen ourselves in the Lord (by thinking on what is true and lovely and biblical) is the extent to which we'll be able to carry the things God has assigned to us. We are hardly in a position to rescue others if only a slight breeze knocks us over. And if we have one foot in the world and one in the Kingdom, our spiritual footing will be too unstable to allow us to steady others.

> Therefore strengthen the hands which hang down, and the feeble knees, and make straight paths for your feet, so that what is lame may not be dislocated, but rather be healed. (Hebrews 12:12–13 NKJV)

We need to pay attention to the frigid drafts that blow through our soul. We need to find the source of our exposure and shut the door so God's Word will remain in us. But isn't it normal to experience cold nights of the soul while living here on earth? Absolutely. It's normal, but we have access to something better. Shut the windows of worry, fear, and unbelief! Seal up the openings of bad attitudes and low perspectives.

> Now may the Lord of peace himself give you peace at all times and in every way. The Lord be with all of you. (2 Thessalonians 3:16 NIV; also see Philippians 4:6–7)

But it's not enough to shut the windows and the doors to keep out the cold. We must fill our mind with God's thoughts and promises. The Bible warns us to be alert to the Enemy's schemes because the mind is a fertile place. Without intervention, the seeds of death and destruction will grow there. Yet with careful attention, that very same soil can conceive dreams and miracles.

Renewing our mind means turning over the soil, pulling the weeds, and planting new seeds daily. It's about shoring up our mind's boundaries so that our thoughts consistently agree with what God wants to do in and through us.

We often don't realize the impact our repetitive thought patterns have. They pave pathways in our brain, making it easier to default to them. Consistent thoughts actually form grooves in our mind, making us instinctively think a certain way.

> Brain researchers now know, from observing positron emission topography (PET) scans of people imagining or watching various scenes, that the brain reacts very similarly to real, watched, and imagined experiences. *At a neurological level, it doesn't really know the difference.* The brain also develops neural pathways that reflect *frequent-use patterns* and builds

synaptic connections *that support habitual trains of thought.* So the idea is that by visualizing a positive experience intensely and regularly enough, you may be able to develop a mental and emotional infrastructure that can support and process it in reality[2] (emphasis mine).

The world has borrowed this biblical concept, called it "positive thinking," and made it into a religion. This dangerous practice denies Christ and exalts man's thoughts; that's a recipe for disaster.

Even so, we cannot turn our back on something the Bible says is essential to our victory! There is both scientific evidence and biblical proof that our thoughts matter. They affect our outlook, our posture, our perspective, and literally our health. They drive the momentum of our life; they lead us into places of freedom or captivity. If we're serious about freedom, we must be serious about taking our thoughts captive and making them *obedient to Christ.*

Just as God keeps Satan on a short leash, we too need to keep our negative thoughts on a short leash. In fact, we need to *demolish* every argument that exalts itself above Christ's influence in our life. We need to put every wandering thought into prison and leave it there. Either our thoughts roam free or we do. We can't have it both ways.

Cultivating a healthy thought life requires our willingness to battle for it. This takes focused living, prayerful practice, diligence, and self-control. It also requires a regular intake of God's Word. But the return on our investment is immeasurable. We are quite literally transformed when we change the way we think (see Romans 12:2).

So how do we take every thought captive? Here are a few suggestions:

Turn your back on anxious thoughts. As simple as this sounds, it works. The moment you sense an anxious or defeating thought arise, put it under your feet! Turn your back on worry and your face toward Christ. Just say no to thoughts that weaken you. It'll make your day.

Find the open door. If your attitude toward others is chilly, ask the Lord to search your heart. Find the open door and shut it. If your passion for the suffering wanes and your love for them grows cold, find the source of the draft and shut the door. Draw near to the fire of God's fierce love; your heart will burn for the things of God once again.

Take Scripture in small sections. Often when our thoughts run wild, they rarely run deep. So instead of trying to read four chapters of the Bible in one sitting, find a verse or two and hold them close. Think about them. Ponder their meaning. Apply them to your life. Picture moving an heirloom into your favorite room. Now picture placing God's priceless Word in a prominent place in your mind. Look upon those words from time to time. Cherish them. Don't allow them to be snatched away from you.

Acknowledge God's presence throughout the day. God is always with us. Daily the heavens pour forth speech. Daily new mercies lie at our door. And every moment of every day, God engages in our life's details. If you need to, acknowledge His presence on the hour and thank Him for something every time. Think about His love. Enjoy the idea that He's got you covered. Think more about what you possess in Him than what's missing from your life right now.

Pray Scripture prayers out loud. The Bible says that faith comes from hearing the Word of God. When Kevin and I started praying Scripture aloud, something significant changed in our lives. It was like a megavitamin for the soul! Find a few Scripture passages that speak to you and write them as a prayer. Eventually those prayers will form pathways in your heart, mind, and soul, and they'll flow right off of your tongue. Instead of defaulting to worry, you'll default to prayer. Praying Scripture *out loud* drowns out every lesser thought. It's a powerful exercise!

Raise your level of expectation. God is always good and always up to something. Instead of assuming things won't work out, expect that they will (see Romans 8:28). A captivity mind-set keeps you working under a heavy load with minimal expectation and minimal results. On the other hand, a Kingdom mind-set compels you to work from a place of abundance and focuses you on our more-than-enough God. He is able to make all grace abound to you so that in all things, at all times, we'll have more than enough to be generous on every occasion!

 **_Faithful Lord,_**

Thank You for the gift of my mind. Help me to be a great steward of my thoughts. Help me to meditate on what is true and beautiful and right. Strengthen me so that I may stand strong against the thoughts that weaken me. Show me the openings in my life that make me vulnerable to captivity and defeat. Transform me this year into a totally new person by helping me to think differently! I reject a spirit of fear and embrace a spirit of power, love, and sound mind. Finally, renew my mind in such a way that compels me to think of and pray for those who suffer. Burden my heart with what burdens Yours.

And now, Lord, I pray for every child slave and child soldier. I cannot even fathom how confused and wounded they must be. Please, Lord, answer my prayer and miraculously put godly, kind people in their lives to love them and nurture them when they need it most. Visit them in their dreams so they might know You to be a God of love. Set them free, renew their minds, and heal every part of them. In Jesus' name, I pray. Amen.

initiate your freedom

1. Read Psalm 119:16. In what ways do you delight in God's principles? Write them down. In what ways do you hang on to God's Word? Write them down. Write a prayer asking God to call you to a new level of faith.

2. Think about the times you've embraced a "captivity spirit" but then moved to a Kingdom perspective. What changed? Maybe you still embrace the lesser perspective. Read 2 Corinthians 9:8–15 and then reread it. Get a feel for what an abundant life would look like operating in and through you. Now write down your "abundant life vision."

3. Read 1 John 2:20, 24. Verse 20 declares that you know the truth. Write down some of the most profound truths you know. Now, based on verse 24, compose a personal declaration of how you plan to see to it —*that God's Word remains in you.*

4. Read Psalm 139:23. Spend some time praying this verse and then listen to what God whispers to your heart. What negative, defeating, or wretched thoughts keep you from remaining in Christ? Write them down.

5. Read Philippians 4:8–9 slowly. Pick one of the standards from this verse. For the rest of the day, ask God to refine your thoughts accordingly (e.g., admirable, praiseworthy, true).

"We know that things are out of control.
We know that as humans we can do only little things.
So we humble ourselves, and it is God who shows up.
He is everything. He is in control."

—IJM INVESTIGATOR, SOUTH ASIA

ALLOWING GOD
TO REDUCE US

I am the true grapevine, and my Father is the gardener. He cuts off every branch of mine that doesn't bear fruit, and he prunes the branches that do bear fruit so they will produce even more. —JOHN 15:1–2

God's discipline is always perfect. His love is infinite and His wisdom is infallible. His chastenings are never the result of whim, but always for our profit.[1] —WILLIAM MACDONALD

One of my heroes of the faith is Catherine Booth, who, alongside her husband, William Booth, founded the Salvation Army in the mid-1800s. Her story reminds me that no eye has seen, no ear has heard, no mind can comprehend what God can do with a heart set on Him (see 1 Corinthians 2:9).

Catherine was painfully shy as a child. She was frail and quite often ill. She more often stayed in and read rather than going out to play with other children. By the time Catherine was twelve, she had read the Bible from cover to cover eight times—out loud.[2]

Catherine might have been poor in health, but she was mighty in spirit. When she was nine, she happened upon an angry mob. People jeered and gawked as a group of men dragged a drunkard to the courthouse. Imagine this frail, shy child marching right into the middle of an angry mob to look into the drunkard's eyes. Read the rest of the account:

> Even though her home was an active outpost of the Temperance Society, Catherine's heart could not condemn the man; she could not stand such treatment of someone so disoriented. So, she marched into the midst of the crowd, right up to the face of the drunkard. Everyone was caught off guard by the boldness of such a small creature, and they stopped dead in their tracks. Catherine came nose to nose with the man, smelling the foulness of his breath and searching his eyes for some hint of humanity behind the empty stare. Then, taking him by the hand, she turned and began to lead him in the same direction the crowd had been taking him. The man's steps became steadier, and the policeman no longer had to tug at him, but walked alongside, merely holding his arm to steady him. Thus, Catherine and the policeman took the man to the lockup, and the crowd lost interest in their taunts. The scene was reminiscent of the biblical account of the accusers of the woman caught in adultery.[3]

Catherine had a passion for the suffering, the poor, and the afflicted, probably because her heart was so acquainted with theirs. Her frail health kept her home from school in her early years, but Catherine finally attended school when she was twelve. Right away her teachers noticed that Catherine was a young woman of conviction, intelligence, and wisdom. Unfortunately, at fourteen, Catherine was again bedridden for three months straight. She used this time to educate herself. Though her world again had shrunk, God was preparing her to change the world.

Years later Catherine married the man God had chosen for her. Together they took society by storm. Whenever William and Catherine saw a need, they sought with God's help to fill it. Under William and Catherine's persevering leadership, the Salvation Army fed the hungry, recovered missing persons, rescued prostitutes, combated human trafficking, found employment for the poor, and ministered salvation to the lost. They *were* the social services of their day.

Throughout their lives, William and Catherine stood strong in the face of opposition, accusation, and sickness . . . and prevailed. Though Catherine experienced seasons of obscurity, she was never out of God's sight. He always had His eye on her. And because of her humble, surrendered heart, God used her in ways far beyond her natural ability. What God did through a young woman frail in health and shy in spirit was quite *super*natural. There's no limit to what God can do through a life totally surrendered to Him.

Why are we talking about "reducing" or "shrinking" in a book that's about enlarging the space on which we live? In order to increase in godly things, we must, over time, decrease in fleshly things. We belong to God Most High, and He reserves the right to lead us into seasons of refinement, obscurity, and pruning. But it's always for a purpose, always for an increased level of freedom and fruitfulness.

> You didn't choose me. I chose you. I appointed you to go and produce lasting fruit, so that the Father will give you whatever you ask for, using my name. (John 15:16)

Imagine making such an impact in this world that it continues to bear fruit long after you're gone. You and I have a divine appointment to make such an impact. Unfortunately, many totally miss their appointment. But God has His eye on us. If we're willing to trust Him, He's willing to use us in astonishing ways. However, producing world-changing fruit requires deep pruning. God reduces us to bring a greater increase through us.

Sometimes God reduces us through discipline. Until we see Jesus face-to-face, we need direction and correction to keep us on track. Since our Good Shepherd leads us with such loving-kindness, His guiding presence should bring us great comfort. *Even when I walk through the darkest valley, I will not be afraid, for you are close beside me. Your rod and your staff protect and comfort me* (Psalm 23:4).

No longer will the poor be name-less—no more humiliation for the humble. (PSALM 9:18 MSG)

Our loving, protective Father usually corrects us privately first. But if we are unwilling to heed His gentle nudges, He'll allow us to make our mistakes in the presence of witnesses. He'll use whatever means necessary to get our attention because He's interested in extracting from us what the Enemy intends to use against us. He disciplines those He loves. *No discipline seems pleasant at the time, but painful. Later on, however, it produces a harvest of righteousness and peace for those who have been trained by it* (Hebrews 12:11 NIV).

> The purpose of God's chastening is not punitive but creative . . . The fire which is kindled is not a bonfire, blazing heedlessly and unguardedly, and consuming precious things; it is a refiner's fire, and the Refiner sits by it, and He is firmly and patiently and gently bringing holiness out of carelessness and stability out of weakness. God is always creating even when He is using the darker means of grace. He is producing the fruits and flowers of the Spirit. His love is always in quest of lovely things.[4]

Other times, God seems to reduce us for no *apparent* reason. Our walk of faith is thriving, our ministry is expanding, the wind is at our back, and suddenly . . . things melt into nothing. We stop in our tracks, look over our shoulder to see if anybody noticed our sudden lack of momentum, and wonder, *Did I just miss something here?*

These are the seasons of divine pruning. This is where the Lord takes His shears and cuts back some branches that show the most promise. It's painful. It seems a senseless waste of time in light of the need and opportunity out there. Worst of all, God seems agonizingly unconcerned with our apparent understanding of the times.

It took me more than a few pruning seasons to learn that it hurts less when I sit still. At first I'd frantically try to catch all of the leaves falling off of my freshly pruned branch. I tried pumping some of my own life into a dead bough. You can imagine how well that worked. Finally, I learned to be still and to know that He is God. As I leaned into the arms of my Beloved, I learned to trust Him more. And as I learned to trust Him more, I grew to love Him more.

Eventually I got to a place where I loved God so much that I only wanted what He wanted for me. And just when I found rest in the purifying process, the season ended and new things opened up for me. Unbelievable things. Opportunities I never could have secured on my own. Amazingly, I was prepared for these new places not because I had been busy preparing, but because I had been still in the shearing. Bruce Wilkinson describes this process perfectly in his book *Secrets of the Vine*:

> *The pain of pruning comes now, but the fruit comes later.* Just as in the vineyard, pruning in our lives is seasonal. But the quantity and quality of the future harvest depends on our submission to the Vinedresser now. *Even though the duration, depth, and breadth of pruning seasons will vary, no season lasts indefinitely.* A season is coming, I promise, when you will know that you are no longer under God's shears. Everywhere you look you'll see amazing evidence of personal transformation and expanded ministry for God.[5]

Allow me to address two more scenarios of what it means to be reduced. In our early years of marriage, Kevin and I walked through the worst part of our wilderness journey. I couldn't hear God's voice. Our cupboards were empty, and so was our bank account. The disease I fought took its toll on me. I was only in my twenties but felt as though I was in my nineties.

Then one day everything changed. A woman from my church called me and said, "I know you and your family are really going through it right now, so I prayed for you. God gave me a picture of a platform that He's building with your pain. You'll be speaking from that place someday. So lean in and learn everything you can." Her words flipped a light switch on within me; suddenly I knew God was up to something.

God had turned up the heat in my life so that when the impurities presented themselves, He could extract them. You might be in such a season right now. If so, lean in and learn everything you can. God has plans for you. Don't allow this time to define you. Don't let faithlessness now keep you from arriving at the spacious place God is preparing *you* for later.

Finally, there are times of internal reducing. For the woman who walks closely with the Lord, these happen more frequently. I know they do for me. On the outside we may appear to be "business as usual," but on the inside God is dealing with us. We still go about our day, working through our task list, making our phone calls, and grabbing a bite to eat. But inside, our spirit is being refined.

God may be speaking to us about our tendency toward gossip or cynicism or self-promotion or self-reliance, or simply about our unbelief. First He speaks and we listen. Then we hear those same words in a song, or see them on a magazine cover at the checkout line, or hear them from a stranger. Everywhere we turn, confirmation is there. And it's painful. While we function on the outside, our spirit groans on the inside. But we listen, and every chance we get, we pray, we repent, and we thank God for the mercy to begin again. These are times when His rod and staff truly are a comfort.

Why do we need to endure these reducing, refining times? We endure because we are called to be like Christ, and we have things to do in this world. To really care about the poor, the slave, and the young girl sold into sex trafficking, we need courage, conviction, and compassion. To take some of the responsibility for life's inequalities, we need a complete overhaul of our selfish suburban mind-set. We cannot sustain such conviction if we are not changed from the inside out.

We have nothing to impart if Christ doesn't first impart it to us. In ourselves we are a bundle of self-sins: selfishness, self-awareness, self-promotion, self-loathing, and self-condemnation. When our imagined rights are stepped on, we rise up. When our fears confront us, we shrink back.

But when Christ lives within us, we step out. And we love and minister with a perspective and a value system that are not of this earth.

There's a vast difference between shrinking back and decreasing in Christ. Shrinking back implies fear, selfishness, or false humility. But decreasing actually means increasing in Christ. Our focus is on the "more of Christ in us" than on what's being burned away.

Some people think that to "decrease" is simply to declare "I'm a wretch" a little bit louder. But to truly decrease is to move into the bigger and more beautiful things of Christ so that they might supernaturally become a more natural part of us.

The focus is always on Christ. When Christ increases in us, we have more to give away, more to impart, and less need for human approval. It's a gloriously free place to be.

 **_Pure and holy God,_**

Oh, how I want to be like You! Purify my heart, my motives, and my ambitions! Give me a renewed perspective and a much deeper conviction to live like You. I will trust You in times of abundance. I will trust You in times of refining and pruning. You have my heart and I want what You want for me. I can't imagine a greater honor than to have my fruit bearing fruit long after I'm gone. More of You in me, Lord! Have Your way in my life.

And now, Lord, I lift up every single young girl who is curled up on a brothel floor. Her world is small and horrid. Oh, God, I ask You to intervene! Bring her out to a spacious place! Protect those who come to her rescue. Bless their families for making such a sacrifice. Move heaven and earth to deliver these girls, because that's the kind of God You are. I believe You will hear me and answer this prayer! In Jesus' name, I pray. Amen.

1. Read John 15:1 and take a moment to pray, "Lord, show me the branches in my life that aren't bearing fruit. Where am I wasting my time or serving out of obligation instead of because You asked me to?" Listen for His voice. Write down what you hear.
   • How about when God prunes a branch that is bearing fruit? It's painful and disillusioning. If you're going through such a time, ask Him for faith and perspective. He'll give it to you.

2. Read John 15:2. Notice how the act of cutting off and pruning could look very much the same—at least from a distance. Your pruning process may look to others like God's discipline. What's your instinctive reaction to that response? What's the solution?

3. Read John 15:4 and list some tangible ways that you cultivate a lifestyle that allows you to *remain in Him.*

4. You're a little more than halfway through this journey. Has your perspective changed in any way? If so, write it down.

5. Read John 15:5 and list some ways you envision *bearing much fruit*, fruit that surpasses your time on earth. Follow this list with a prayer asking God to fulfill the desires of your heart.

"When it comes to work of justice, God is the one who does everything, not me. A former colleague gave me this analogy: It's like when a mom makes cookies with her child. After the cookies are baked, the child says, 'Yes, I made these cookies,' even though the child made more of a mess and mistakes. But the mother is happy to have him take credit and celebrate the cookies. Often, because of our innocence, what we make might turn out well. But it is God who is doing everything."

—RICHARD, ATTORNEY, IJM SOUTH ASIA

15

HONORING GOD

Taste and see that the Lord is good. Oh, the joys of those who take refuge in him! Fear the Lord, you his godly people. For those who fear him will have all they need. —PSALM 34:8–9

There are no days when God's fountain does not flow.[1]

—RICHARD OWEN ROBERTS

Peter ran until his lungs screamed *for air. Then, totally deflated, he collapsed to the ground, held his stomach, and heaved uncontrollable sobs. The veins in his neck bulged as he cried into the night, "My Savior, my Jesus! What have I done? Oh, Lord, I am finished! How will You ever forgive me?" Peter rolled over onto his stomach, put his face in the dirt, and pounded the ground with his fists. His tears mixed with the dirt and muddied his face, but he didn't notice. Grief overtook Peter. His best friend and Savior—the One who transformed his life—needed him now more than ever. And Peter pretended not to know Him. Peter pulled his knees up under him and with his forehead on the ground he began to pray through fits of tears. He stayed there all night.**

Peter, one of Jesus' best friends, denied even knowing Him. I've read that account over and over again, and every time I do, I ache for Peter. I relate to Peter. I have the best of intentions at times, but

**My imaginative portrayal of Peter's denial of Christ*

my sense of self-protection is strong. Oh, if not for the patient grace of God, where would I be?

Peter loved Jesus and Jesus loved Peter. Peter was a man of faith and action . . . albeit hasty action at times. Even so, Peter was in Jesus' inner circle. When Jesus first approached Peter to follow Him, Peter didn't hesitate. He immediately left his net, his livelihood, and his father's business.

When Jesus walked on the water, it was Peter who dared to ask to join Jesus in the miracle. If Jesus said something Peter didn't understand, Peter boldly said, "Explain what you mean." When Jesus asked the disciples, *Who do people say that the Son of Man is?* (Matthew 16:13), Peter, by the Holy Spirit's power, declared, *You are the Messiah, the Son of the living God* (verse 16).

To paint a balanced picture, Peter was also the one who was overly hasty on several occasions. When Jesus spoke of going to the cross, it was Peter who jumped in the way and said, "May it never be!" He was of such an earthly mind-set that Jesus rebuked him. When the soldiers arrested Jesus in the garden of Gethsemane, Peter drew his sword and sliced off the ear of the high priest's servant. Jesus healed the man and told Peter to put away his sword.

Another time, Peter, James, and John joined Jesus up on the mountain. Jesus' appearance changed; His face shone like the sun and his clothes became dazzling white (see Matthew 17:1–2). Suddenly Elijah and Moses appeared and began talking with Jesus. And what was Peter's response?

Peter broke in, "Master, this is a great moment! What would you think if I built three memorials here on the mountain—one for you, one for Moses, one for Elijah?" While he was going on like this, babbling, a light-radiant cloud enveloped them, and sounding from deep within the cloud a voice: *This is my Son, marked by my love, focus of my delight. Listen to him* (Matthew 17:4–5 MSG).

Peter's response was to say and do something! And right in the midst of his self-striving efforts, the God of the Universe uttered these words: *"This is my dearly loved Son, who brings me great joy. Listen to him." The disciples were terrified and fell face down on the ground* (Matthew 17:5–6, emphasis mine).

In the presence of the living God, Peter was reduced. Time and time again, Peter ate his humble pie. But he kept coming back to his Savior, and over time he was transformed into a mighty man of faith who would change the world.

Let's look at one more scene. This encounter reveals a transformed Peter. Others' opinions no longer mattered; neither did self-protection. Peter fiercely and powerfully honored God, and God in return honored Peter with great authority and boldness.

Peter and John were thrown in jail for preaching the gospel and ministering to the needy. When they were brought before the council of elders and religious leaders, Peter didn't hesitate. With absolute clarity and power, Peter responded to their inquisition:

> Then Peter, filled with the Holy Spirit, said to them, "Rulers and elders of our people, are we being questioned today because we've done a good deed for a crippled man? Do you want to know how he was healed? Let me clearly state to all of you and to all the people of Israel that he was healed by the powerful name of Jesus Christ the Nazarene, the man you crucified but whom God raised from the dead. For Jesus is the one referred to in the Scriptures, where it says, 'The stone that you builders rejected has now become the cornerstone.' There is salvation in no one else! God has given no other name under heaven by which we must be saved." (Acts 4:8–12)

Talk about authority. Peter's mistakes were behind him. He'd been reduced and then restored. God worked mightily through him. And how did others respond? Let's look at the following verse:

The members of the council were amazed when they saw the boldness of Peter and John, for they could see that they were ordinary men with no special training in the Scriptures. They also recognized them as men who had been with Jesus. (Acts 4:13)

Years ago, I went through a major refining period (one of several in my life). My dreams were on hold, my character flaws were before me, and God was dealing with them one by one. I felt as though I was a sailor created to sail the open seas who was confined to the beach to pick up the garbage that the tide washed in. Day in and day out, I walked the shores, picked up the garbage, and watched as the other sea lovers gleefully sailed out to sea.

I knew I could quit looking at my personal garbage and abandon this whole character-cleansing process. If I wanted, I could make something happen on my own. I had a free will. But I wanted God's best for me. I wanted my life's fruit to nourish people long after I passed into eternity. And more than anything, I wanted to be more like Jesus.

My true resolve was tested one day when I saw my dreams flying on someone else's sail. I served in a ministry that didn't seem to fit my primary gifts and strengths; it wasn't an easy place for me to be. Yet I was right where God wanted me—in a stretching, humbling, learning-to-obey-even-when-it-didn't-suit-me mode. I felt called to both a speaking and writing ministry, and although I already was a speaker, even that ministry was on the altar. Submission and obedience beckoned a response from me. Since I wanted everything God designed for me, He needed access to every part of me. I struggled to put it all on the table, every hope, dream, aspiration, and desire. Not an easy thing to do.

God is smart, though. Obviously more of "me" had to go before He could take me where He wanted me.

There I was in my refining season, serving and minding my

business, when a woman began telling me all of the wonderful things going on in her ministry. She couldn't keep up with all of the requests for her to speak. On top of that, someone approached her about writing a book. Surprised and excited, she blurted out, "I've never even thought of writing a book, and just like that, I was asked to write one! What are the chances?"

I smiled at her and died inside. My dreams were on her sail and it was flapping in my face. The wind was at her back and it was messing up my hair. I was completely jealous and even frustrated. I'm a bit nauseated about being so honest with you, but I'm making an important point here.

The next morning during my prayer time, I apologized to the Lord for my attitude. I surrendered my dreams once again. I trusted Him to forgive me and to renew my resolve to obey Him amidst a difficult time. What I didn't know was that I was about to be knocked over by His response: *If the closest you ever get to a speaking and writing ministry is simply to pray for that other woman's success, will you do that for Me? Do you love Me enough to serve Me in this capacity: to humble yourself before Me by being her behind-the-scenes prayer support—even if she never knows it?*

I was aghast. I didn't see that coming. I couldn't even answer right away. I crawled to the floor, put my face to the ground, took a deep breath, and prayed, "Um, I'm going to have to get back to You on that one." At that moment, I didn't have a "yes" in me. I was happy to pray for that woman, but I wanted to pray for me too. I so strongly sensed that God had called me to write and speak that the thought of it all coming to nothing broke my heart. For three days I wrestled with my will, hopes, and selfish ambitions.

Finally, on the third day, I knelt before the Lord, put my head to the floor, and said, "Yes, Lord. I will do that. You have me. All of me. I don't want one thing that You don't want for me. Besides, it doesn't matter what I *do* for You if it's done to honor me. This cannot be about my ambitions and goals; it's about Your Kingdom work and getting it done in the best way possible. I am Yours. Do with me what You will."

I lifted my head and my heart flooded with an overwhelming sense of God's peace and presence. I loved Him more at that moment than I had in a long time. I kept my word and prayed for the woman with the flapping sail. But that only lasted a short time. After a while, God completely released me from the burden to intercede for her. I knew it was time to move on.

The Bible says that pride goes before a fall and that humility precedes honor (see Proverbs 29:23). Although refining times are difficult, they are for our protection. When we honor the Lord in the refining, He blesses us before a watching world. Not that our honor is the point; His honor and our submission are.

We can choose to jump out of the refiner's fire with our pride intact. But the same pride that helps us save face will cause us to stumble and fall flat on our face. When we humbly bow before God, the Lord considers it a great *honor* to reside within us. Honestly, it's hard to fathom the mixture of our awesome God's majesty and humility, but that is who He is.

> He lifts the poor from the dust and the needy from the garbage dump. He sets them among princes, placing them in seats of honor. For all the earth is the Lord's, and he has set the world in order.
>
> (1 Samuel 2:8)

The high and lofty one who lives in eternity, the Holy One, says this: "I live in the high and holy place with those whose spirits are contrite and humble. I restore the crushed spirit of the humble and revive the courage of those with repentant hearts." (Isaiah 57:15)

What I can't get over is that God allows us to carry things so dear to Him—His glory, His power, His Holy Spirit, His message to a lost and dying world—knowing that we will make mistakes, take the credit, and even occasionally miss the mark. He'll happily use us on Monday knowing we're about to blow it on Tuesday. He knows how imperfect and self-centered we can be, yet He entrusts heaven's greatness to His beloved ones.

Like a grandma who unfathomably allows her little grandchild to carry a family heirloom, the Lord places in our hands a God-sized calling with a measure of His glory. He surrounds us with grace, mercy, and all of the supernatural help we need. Then He leads us on, allowing us to join Him in this Kingdom work. What an absolute honor!

And then . . . He rewards *us* for having the faith and the courage to work alongside Him! He knows how fickle we are and yet He makes our heart His home. Amazing love, how can it be?

What happens when we honor God? God is pleased. And we are changed. We step into a realm of Kingdom reality that cannot be realized any other way. When we honor God, a glorious exchange takes place. First we are reduced in His presence and God removes what needs to go. Then we are lifted up again.

It's almost as if our spiritual DNA changes in the process. We begin to care far more about His glory, His people, and His burdens than our own. Our world goes from being as small as a postage stamp to as large as a map of landscapes we may never visit. We don't have that kind of conviction within ourselves, but when God invades our little world, it becomes a big world.

We honor God because He deserves all that we are and more. But no one can outgive our Lord. When we give Him the reverence and honor due His name, we experience the ultimate paradox: *we* are lifted up and honored by a gushing, proud heavenly Father. When we honor God first and foremost, He uses us in ways far beyond us.

So humble yourselves under the mighty power of God, and at the right time he will lift you up in honor. (1 Peter 5:6)

Like Peter and John, we will speak with greater authority and serve with greater sincerity. And when others question why we are able to serve in a way that's bigger than we are, they'll conclude that we've been with Jesus. I wouldn't want to live a day without the Lord Jesus, would you?

 ***Honorable Lord,***

You are everything to me. Thank You for taking such a divine interest in my life and in my freedom. I humbly bow before You now, and I honor You as my King, my Lord, my Savior, my Deliverer, and my dearest Friend. I know the best way I can honor You is by doing what You ask of me. Give me faith, courage, and conviction to tend to Your work while I live here on earth. Blessed be Your name.

And now, Lord, I pray for every young girl who has been dishonored by evil men and women. Restore her soul. Release her from captivity. Stretch out Your hand, rescue her, and lead her to a place where she is honored and loved. Heal her in every way, Lord. Oh, Father, I ask that You crush the plans of the Enemy and establish the plans of Your people! Move in power in these desperate times. Hear my prayer! Amen.

1. One way to honor God is to honor others above yourself. This isn't about considering yourself less than others, but about being *more* in Christ. Read Romans 12:10 and prayerfully list those whom God is asking you to honor publicly and privately.

2. Another way to honor God is to do what He says. He clearly commands us to advocate for the poor and the defenseless. Read Proverbs 14:31 and continually ask God to awaken your compassion for those the world discards. Write a prayer for them.

3. We honor God by acknowledging Him. Read Exodus 17:15 and think about the most recent time God moved on your behalf. Buy a candle, a cross, or something else that reminds you of how God moved. Put it somewhere in your home where you can see it. As you put your visual reminder in place, pray, "Lord, I acknowledge that You are good. You are faithful, and You'll be faithful again today. I honor You with my life."

4. Honor God by radically serving and trusting Him. Read Acts 16:16–34 and follow Paul and Silas through these verses.
   • Why were they jailed?
   • They were severely beaten, shackled, and placed in the deepest, darkest cell. Imagine these men of God going through such a thing.
   • Their response? They worshiped. Look at verse 25 again. People are watching how you handle adversity. What do they see?
   • Reread verse 26. Others were set free because Paul and Silas honored God. Stop here and pray that those watching you would likewise be influenced.
   • Read verses 27–34 and remember this: God's call on your life is formidable. The strongest shackles and the deepest prison cannot shut down the power of God in you!

5. Honor God by giving Him the sacrifice of praise. Read Hebrews 13:15. This exercise may be the toughest of all, but when you honor God amidst your pain, He thinks it's a big deal. When the cupboards are empty or your dreams are flapping in the wind—and you praise Him for His faithfulness—all of heaven notices. God deserves your trust even in the worst of times, and He will, in due time, lift you up. Write a prayer that costs you something—a sacrifice of praise.

"A friend once said this to me: 'Sometimes people are more preoccupied with building their own kingdoms than they are with building God's Kingdom.' I believe that bringing freedom, justice, and healing to girls trapped in the sex trade is a powerful way for us to get beyond our selfish preoccupations and advance God's Kingdom."

—JON, FIELD OFFICE DIRECTOR, IJM SOUTH ASIA

16

EMBRACING GOD'S
HEART FOR JUSTICE

I will search for the lost and bring back the strays. I will bind
up the injured and strengthen the weak, but the sleek and the
strong I will destroy. I will shepherd the flock with justice.

—EZEKIEL 34:16 NIV

God desires to shine light into the dark places of injustice, and
he does that through us. . . . Justice is not optional for Chris-
tians. It is central to God's heart and thus critical to our rela-
tionship with God.[1]
—GARY HAUGEN

On the night before we left Guatemala, our team crammed
into an IJM staffer's apartment and enjoyed some wonderful
Guatemalan cuisine. We weren't ready to say good-bye to these wonderfully kind and humble people who awed us with their bravery.

Just when the night seemed to be winding down, Pablo Villeda,
IJM Guatemala's field office director, took a large picture off the
wall. He set up his projector and showed us a video clip of an arrest
in progress.

"Who is this?" we asked. We learned that the man—a security officer, no less—had molested a little girl in front of her younger sister.

In a country where the average wage is about $7 a day, this man
held a steady, respectable, decent-paying job, one that involved

enforcing the law. Because of his standing in the community, he assumed he'd get away with violating a beautiful young child.

Thankfully, he didn't.

The next morning our team boarded a bus for one last excursion before heading to the airport. Again the bus took us on twists and turns through the countryside. We stepped off the bus in front of a dilapidated shack tucked away in the hills. The chickens clucked, the dogs barked, and a soft breeze blew through the trees.

We were at the little girl's home—the one who had been abused by the security guard. Her mom worked hard all morning to make us a marvelous breakfast. She came out to greet us and graciously welcomed us into their world. We were incredibly honored to be there. As our host and a couple of our team members put the finishing touches on breakfast, the rest of us played with the kids as Tracy, an IJM intern, translated for us.

It was time to pray over our breakfast of fried plantains, corn tortillas, and scrambled eggs with vegetables. At that moment the little girl's mother—who was obviously shy—stepped up to say something. With Tracy at her side, she broke down and sobbed.

Tracy pulled her close and encouraged her to take her time. Through her tears and through Tracy's translation, the girl's mother looked at us and began to speak. She thanked us profusely for getting justice for her little girl. I was tempted to look over my shoulder to see if she was talking to someone else. But she looked at me, then at Kevin, and then at each of our other team members—one by one.

She knew we were IJM supporters; that's why we were on this trip. But we hadn't actually rescued the little girl. The IJM lawyers and social workers were the heroes here. As far as she was concerned, *we had* rescued her daughter. Over and over she thanked us and blessed us, and her sweet little girl wrapped her arms around each of us, repeating the words *Gracias, gracias.*

Through her tears, the young girl's mother said, "We have justice now. My little girl is not afraid anymore. She's beginning to smile again, and she plays with her sister. We didn't think anyone would help us, but you did. We thank God for you."

At first I didn't feel comfortable receiving thanks for what the IJM workers did on this family's behalf. But the longer I sat there, and with every hug I received, I finally concluded that we did have something to do with this rescue. Our money and our prayers actually made a difference. Wonder upon wonders.

The phrase "your gifts make a difference" sounds cliché, yet the reality of those words confronted me when I had to reply to my gracious host and to her daughter, "You are so very welcome. We are honored to help." That encounter for me, narrowed the gap between giving a gift and saving a life.

Looking into the eyes of those poor yet grateful people made me want to invest even greater amounts of money, prayers, and time—as a way of life.

What a way to conclude a life-changing trip. On our first day in Guatemala, we visited government officials and witnessed God's influence through the work of IJM in the halls of power. The sense of reverence and respect around us was tangible.

Now on our last day, when we visited that tiny shack nestled in the hills, we saw God there too. I realized that God knew all about this little home and precious family. He knew their address and He heard their cries for help. And our friends at IJM stepped up and answered the call.

My life is different now. I read the Scriptures through a justice lens. I sense God's burning heart for the voiceless, and I hear—loud and clear—His clarion call for us to be His hands and feet to a world in need.

In every way possible, God communicates His heart for justice. In fact, justice is such a big deal to God that it's the *foundation* of His throne.

The work of God's people on behalf of the poor must be more than a periodic prayer or a check written to a relief agency. God commands us to do as He does by actively defending the rights of the needy, advocating for them, and coming to their aid when we see them oppressed, discriminated against, or mistreated. We must speak up for the marginalized if, because they are poor, they are treated unfairly in the line at the grocery store or at a restaurant. We are God's ambassadors, acting on His behalf to defend those who are violated.[2]

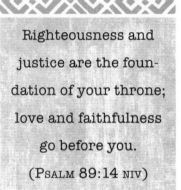

Righteousness and justice are the foundation of your throne; love and faithfulness go before you.

(PSALM 89:14 NIV)

Speak up for those who cannot speak for themselves, for the rights of all who are destitute. Speak up and judge fairly; defend the rights of the poor and needy. (Proverbs 31:8–9 NIV)

These are turbulent times. People and organizations are being sifted and shaken. Our once secure, once prosperous nation now seems vulnerable and fragile. Today's atmosphere is ripe for people to start stampeding over the rights of others to grab for themselves.

But we will not be shaken. Psalm 112 reminds us that we can face the future confidently and fearlessly. Now is the time to be consistent in our intimacy with Jesus, so we can be strong in the Lord and strong for justice. No longer can our self-protective desires trump the times. God has a divine call for each of us, one that requires faith and courage, hope and love. May we be known not for how many material goods we accumulate or for how well we insulate ourselves from the world's pain, but for how well we know *Him*.

> Boast in this alone: that they truly know me and understand that I am the Lord who demonstrates unfailing love and who brings justice and righteousness to the earth, and that I delight in these things. I, the Lord, have spoken! (Jeremiah 9:24)

Jesus was gentle with the sinner who knew she was a sinner, but He was tough on the self-righteous Pharisee and even tougher on the conniving, manipulative person who thought nothing of stepping on the rights of others (often the Pharisee *was* the unjust one). Read the Gospels and notice the two extreme sides of Jesus' personality— tough and tender. Oh, how I love Him!

It's easy to think of injustice in the worst terms (human trafficking, abduction, slavery, murder, etc.). The Bible points out that we *should* think of injustice in this way. We must not put our head in the sand.

But the Lord hates lesser injustices just as much. He hates it when people slander and gossip. He hates it when people are quick to manipulate others. He hates pride, lying, and divisiveness. And if you've been on the receiving end of one of these, you know how terrible it feels. Jesus knows too.

Our Savior and King received no justice. Jesus endured every evil intention listed in the verses below. He knows what is in the heart of man, and He will one day balance the scales.

> What are worthless and wicked people like? They are constant liars, signaling their deceit with a wink of the eye, a nudge of the foot or the wiggle of fingers. Their perverted hearts plot evil, and they constantly

stir up trouble. But they will be destroyed suddenly, broken in an instant beyond all hope of healing. There are six things the Lord hates— no, seven things he detests: haughty eyes, a lying tongue, hands that kill the innocent, a heart that plots evil, feet that race to do wrong, a false witness who pours out lies, a person who sows discord in a family. (Proverbs 6:12–19)

God is our defender. He will vindicate us from wretched injustices. He will set the record straight. He will get back what was stolen from us. And for our own missteps and mistakes, He'll forgive us if we ask Him to.

Now is not the time to be caught up in the petty dramas common among women. We must stand on the side of righteousness even if it means confronting our best friend with a difficult truth or pulling back from a group headed in a direction not intended for us. We may be called to defend someone who once betrayed us. Justice is blind in the issues of right and wrong; it's *supposed* to be no respecter of persons. Our integrity before the Lord matters more than ever. We were made in God's image! And He loves justice.

Today is our chance to honor the Lord's request to stand up for the sake of justice. May His Kingdom come and His will be done amidst every injustice on the earth.

 ***Precious Lord,***

You have made Yourself very clear: You care about the poor and the oppressed and You've entrusted this burden to Your people. Forgive me for the countless ways I've missed You in this area! Thank You for Your kind and gentle patience with my maturing process. Thank You for loving me as I am, and thank You for calling me to things that are beyond me. Fill my heart with a greater passion for the poor. Give me clarity on the issues of justice. Lead me by the power of Your Holy Spirit to make a difference in this world.

And now, Lord, I pray for the millions of men, women, and children who are nameless to the world, but not to You. By Your mighty power, bring them justice! Crush the power of the Enemy and establish the plans of Your people! Father, hear my cry and move on behalf of every victim of injustice in this world. Provoke me to pray as often as You need me to. Jesus, may Your righteousness come to bear on these situations that the victims may receive justice and sing for joy once again. In Jesus' name, I pray. Amen.

1. Read Psalm 11:7. This verse speaks of who the Lord is and what He loves. Use three words or more to describe righteousness and justice.

   • Think about a person whom you absolutely adore. Now think about something that he or she absolutely loves. Can you imagine being in a devoted relationship with this person while ignoring one of his or her most significant passions? Take a minute to ponder God's love for justice. Think about God and justice long enough so that the two become intertwined. When you think about one, may you think about the other.

   • Now take the last part of the verse and consider what it means to God when we embrace His passion for justice. He brings us into His inner circle. He confides in us. He equips us. And He honors us with His presence. Ask God for more courage. Write a prayer.

2. Read Isaiah 56:1. What is God asking you to do today? Think about the upcoming year. In what ways do you sense God asking you to maintain justice? Your call is different than mine. What's the right thing for *you* to do?

3. Read Proverbs 29:7. Write a declaration that you are righteous and that you care about the poor! Even if you feel you have a long way to go (we all do), declare this truth over your life. Believe it by faith.

4. Read Psalm 82:3–4. Take a minute to pray for the godly lawyers, judges, and social workers who fight injustice day in and day out. Ask God to give you a special burden for them.

5. Read Isaiah 30:18 and think about your life for a second. Do you or someone you love need a breakthrough from God? Sit back, close your eyes, and picture Him working on your behalf. Thank Him by faith that He is. Enjoy simply waiting in God's presence and resting in His care. He wants justice for you too.

6. Pick one Sunday a month, or one song every Sunday, and worship on behalf of the oppressed, the suffering, and the slave. When you sing words of rescue and redemption, sing wholeheartedly on behalf of those in need. You'll experience a new level of worshipful prayer.

"It is despair that has the facts wrong. In the long run, it is always the tyrants and bullies who end up on the ash heap of history. Sometimes the moral arc of the universe is long indeed. Sometimes unbearably long. But on both small and epic scales, it does bend towards justice. And miraculously, God has given into human hands the power to bend it more quickly to its ultimate destination."[3]

—GARY HAUGEN, IJM PRESIDENT AND CEO

17

Taking New Land

How long will you flit here and there, indecisive? How long before you make up your fickle mind? God will create a new thing in this land: A transformed woman will embrace the transforming God! —Jeremiah 31:22 msg

Moving into the land God has waiting for us is not something for the timid or the fearful. It's for people who know that God would not bring us this far in life only to drop us into some black hole.[1] —Jim Cymbala

One day (Jesus) and his disciples got in a boat. "Let's cross the lake," he said. And off they went. It was smooth sailing, and he fell asleep. A terrific storm came up suddenly on the lake. Water poured in, and they were about to capsize. They woke Jesus: "Master, Master, we're going to drown!" Getting to his feet, he told the wind, "Silence!" and the waves "Quiet down!" They did it. The lake became smooth as glass. Then he said to his disciples, "Why can't you trust me?" They were in absolute awe, staggered and stammering, "Who is this, anyway? He calls out to the winds and sea, and they do what he tells them!" (Luke 8:22–25 msg)

Put yourself right in the middle of this day: You're crammed in a fishing boat with a bunch of your friends. You're all Christians. You love Jesus. People know that about you; they identify you as someone connected to Him. You're all in the boat because Jesus said, "Let's go." But then the storm hits. Water spills over the sides of the boat. The whitecaps turn into walls of water, pushing you every which way. The clouds swirl overhead in varying directions. The winds whistle through the air. And Jesus remains silent, peacefully sleeping. Uninvolved. Or so it seems.

You wonder what in the world you were thinking. You're sure you heard Him right, but then did you? You are suddenly more self-aware than God-aware. All you can see is the imminent danger that surrounds you. Would you call out to God with all your might, "Help us, Lord! We're about to drown"? Doesn't that seem like the right thing to do?

The disciples cried out to Jesus in their fear. Jesus rose up and rebuked the storm. Then He asked them, "Why can't you trust me?" In another version of the passage above, Jesus asks, "Where was your faith?" Jesus told His disciples that they were going to the other side of the lake. He had never lied to them before and He wasn't lying now. Jesus wanted more from His closest followers. Jesus wants more from us.

Just as Jesus asked the disciples to get in the boat with Him and cross the lake, He asks us to follow Him to someplace unknown as well. Where do you suppose He wants to lead you?

When the disciples conquered new land with Jesus, they learned more intensely about His power to heal and restore. They understood more deeply about their frailties and weaknesses. And they were offered greater opportunities to help those in need.

So it goes with us. With every inch of new territory God leads us to lay hold of, we gain a greater understanding of what it means to be linked in fellowship with the Most High God. His promises mean more to us than ever before because we need them. Verses such as *For the kingdom of God is not a matter of talk but of power* (1 Corinthians 4:20 NIV) take on new meaning. We rely on His love far more than the favorable opinions of others because we learn just how fickle humans can be (and how steady God is). With new land come increased opportunities to minister to a greater number of people in miraculous, life-changing ways. What an adventure God has for us!

Jesus promised his disciples three things—that they would be completely fearless, absurdly happy and in constant trouble.[2]

—G. K. Chesterton

At some point—if we really want to please God with our faith—we have to get up and go to the next place Jesus has for us. This "get up and go" requires a measure of courage. Along the way, we'll get caught in a storm, and occasionally we'll get pushed back or knocked down. We'll wonder if we heard wrong or if Jesus simply looked away for a moment. In order to persevere, we'll have to reconcile our excuses and fears with what Jesus told us *before* we set out on our adventure. We must remember in the darkness what He told us in the light.

What does your new territory look like? Is God calling you to go on a short-term mission trip or to reach out to your local food pantry? Maybe your new territory is a slower pace of living that allows more room for God. Or perhaps it's a healthier lifestyle, or a greater commitment to your community.

If you and I walk closely with the Lord and spend daily time in His presence; if we immediately respond in faith to the Holy Spirit's guidance within us; if we regularly recite and remember the Lord's promises and commands; if we quickly repent of our sin; and if we humbly accept His divine correction, then we can move forward bravely. We'll know—beyond a shadow of a doubt—that our Lord leads us every step of the way and that nothing—no, nothing—can harm us without His permission.

When the trials do come, we can rest assured that they're filtered through His hands, and we can stand tall and walk on in faith. Times of measured distress bring our fears to the surface. Storms show us what can be shaken within us and what cannot. Sometimes we're stronger than we think. Sometimes we're weaker. It's good for us to know ourselves. It's important for us to trust God because we have great things to do in this life.

God takes us into deep waters, not to drown us but to cleanse us.[3]

As part of my prayer time, I often first pray the "prayer of Jabez" for increased territory *within me.* My prayer goes something like this:

Dear Lord, bless me indeed! Increase Your territory within me. Take up increasing space in my life. Spread out to the right and to the left and secure the land I've given up to fear and pain and mistrust! Turn the light on in the dark corners of my soul; chase out the fears and anxieties that threaten my freedom. Strengthen me in the deepest places, Lord. Help me to secure the borders of my mind that my life may flourish. And may Your mighty hand of power be at work in me and all around me! Keep me from evil, temptation, and pain, from both causing it and enduring it. And may I live out the number of my days in nobility, honor, and freedom.

Then I move to the original prayer author Bruce Wilkinson so eloquently taught in *The Prayer of Jabez.* He encourages us to pray it in our words. Here's my prayer:

Precious Father, please bless me indeed! Enlarge my sphere of influence; let me do more for You for Your name's sake. Help me to love what You love and hate what You hate. Give me a heart to do Your will, and may Your law be written on my heart. May Your Kingdom passion and Calvary love daily increase in my life. Burden my heart with what burdens Yours. Give me a passion for the weak, the hurting, the hungry, and the slave. May

Your hand of power be mightily at work all around me. Keep me from evil and temptation; both causing and enduring it; help me to live out the number of my days in a manner worthy of Your name, Lord. Amen.

Almost every time I speak at a retreat or conference, I ask the women to stretch out their arms. My heart skips a beat every time I look out to a sea of outstretched arms. Then I pace back and forth onstage, making sure every woman knows that this truth is for *her*: "You have a calling on your life! Before you were ever born, God had you in mind. And the plan He designed for you is so out of this world, you'll never accomplish it unless God intervenes. So if everything you're accomplishing is within your reach, your world is too small. Your God is too small.

> You're one happy man when you do what's right, one happy woman when you form the habit of justice.
> (PSALM 106:3 MSG)

"His plan for your life goes far beyond your comfort zone. The very idea of this calling will sometimes make your heart race and your knees weak. It'll take faith to get there and faith to stay there. God's highest and best plan for you is *that* grand. The sad thing is, many, many Christians have lived and died on a plot of land that was far smaller than the promised-land destiny written over their lives; they claimed far fewer resources than were available to them; they lived far beneath their means with regards to faith. God's promise and supply are much greater than they knew."

Since Jesus has appointed us to bear *much* fruit—fruit that will stand the test of time, that will still bear fruit long after we are gone—then we must lay hold of the otherworldly call on our life (see John 15).

The call on your life and mine is altogether glorious, frightening, demanding, and exhilarating. It takes a willing soul to allow God to stretch the boundaries of her comfort zone, to train her to have tough skin while maintaining a tenderized heart. It takes a tenacious soul to shape her thinking in line with God's Word, to refine her core beliefs so that she's no longer limited by her past experiences.

Most men and women don't want to go there. But for the one who is willing, God will do abundantly above and beyond all she could ever dare to ask or think, according to the work she allows Him to do within her (see Ephesians 3:20). And this mind-boggling call will in some form include the sufferings of others.

> "But a beautiful cedar palace does not make a great king! Your father, Josiah, also had plenty to eat and drink. But he was just and right in all his dealings. That is why God blessed him. He gave justice and help to the poor and needy, and everything went well for him. Isn't that what it means to know me?" says the Lord. (Jeremiah 22:15–16)

Faithful Lord,

Thank You for loving me. Thank You for allowing me to do this journey with You. I want nothing more than to please You by my faith. Take me to the new land You have for me. Take me past accusing voices, old fears, and insecurities, and lead me to my next place of promise. Make me bold and brave, courageous and compassionate. Transform me from the inside out so that I am willing to follow wherever You lead. Here I am, Lord, send me.

And now, Lord, I pray for all of the young girls who cannot even imagine a "next place of promise." Visit them in their dreams. Give them visions of hope and expectation. Confuse the plans of their oppressors, and establish the plans of those working on their rescue. Make a way where there seems to be no way. Give them back the land the Enemy has stolen from them. And then take them into their new places of promise. I pray this in Your name. Amen.

1. Read Philippians 2:13 and spend some time in silence before the Lord. Really ponder this verse for a while. Describe some of the ways you're changing. How is God working in you to shape you for His purposes?

2. Read Luke 18:1–5. Can you relate to this woman? What kinds of needs have you brought this persistently before the Lord?
   • How long did you persevere?
   • What was the outcome?

3. Read Luke 18:6–8. Consider what it means to persevere (to bear up under a weight for a certain period of time).
   • Some of the weight we carry is our sin, unbelief, or simple desire to have what we want. Are any of your choices bogging down your faith? Spend some time with the Lord. He'll speak to you.
   • Some of the weight we carry is unfulfilled desires and prolonged waiting for a breakthrough. Are you dealing with any of those? Write them down. Then write a prayer of commitment, stating that you will persist, you will not relent, and you will pray until His promise becomes your reality.

4. Read Ephesians 3:20. God has a next place of promise for you! And to the extent that you allow Him to work His greatness in you, will He work His greatness through you. Ask God to increase His territory within you.

"Before doing something, I think of the pros and cons. Before, if I thought there was a 50 percent chance of success, I would do it—but less than 50 percent, I wouldn't. IJM has transformed me. Now I know if there is a one percent chance, that's more than enough for God. Rather than thinking, *It won't work,* I think, *If there's a one percent chance, try that.*"

—RICHARD, ATTORNEY, IJM SOUTH ASIA

 **18**

Becoming
a Risk Taker

*God doesn't want us to be shy with his gifts, but bold and
loving and sensible.*   —2 TIMOTHY 1:7 MSG

The more we depend on God, the more dependable we find he is.[1]
                                                  —CLIFF RICHARDS

Are you a born risk taker? I tend to be more of a play-it-safe girl, although my mom insists otherwise. She tells me that I *was* a big-time risk taker as a child. One day when we were at my brother's ballgame, she turned around and I was gone. I was only four years old at the time. My poor mom frantically ran around the park looking for me, asking others if they'd seen a chubby little girl with a pixie haircut. But I was nowhere to be found, and my mom was beside herself.

Suddenly she heard a family laughing and turned to look at them. They were on the other side of the park, enjoying a nice family picnic. With a blanket spread beneath them and a couple of buckets of Kentucky Fried Chicken before them, they laughed and ate and soaked up the summer day. My mom squinted her eyes, looked a little closer, and found *me* sitting on the blanket with the picnicking family! She ran across the park, stopped short of the blanket, and with winded breath asked, "Susie, what do you think you're doing?" I smiled and said, "Momma, meet my new friends." Then I proceeded to name them one by one. Apparently I had wandered over to the family's picnic (maybe I smelled the food) and stood at the edge of their blanket, staring at them. That's one way to get what you want. The strangers were kind enough to invite me to join them. Mission accomplished.

My poor mother has lots of stories such as this one that have convinced her I was a born risk taker. But I still don't see myself that way.

Enough painful, scary things happened to me over time that I became a no-risk kind of girl. I liked to color within the lines. I liked my predictable schedule. I didn't want to open myself up to unknown scenarios that threatened my safe, controlled existence. In fact, for a long time I never wanted to leave the country and I didn't think it was even necessary to leave the state. I'm embarrassed to admit it, but it's true.

For years, I was snug as a bug on my small patch of life. Okay, that's not exactly true. I knew that I was ruled by fear. I hated it, but I didn't know how to conquer my fears and take risks. So I prayed for faraway places from my comfort zone. I gave money to those in need from my comfort zone. I did good things all from my comfort zone.

But God isn't interested in our comfortable lifestyle. Man-made comfort zones make us soft and insignificant. Believers are called out of the comfort zone and into the faith zone. We are *made* for the stretching, reaching, I-don't-know-if-I-can-do-this faith. But God leads us with infinite wisdom and grace, suitable for our strength and maturity level. Safety is a good thing; self-protection, not so much.

As a former fitness instructor, I still love to work out. I'm fascinated by the science of the human body; the more I learn about the intricacies of our systems, the more magnificent God becomes to me. Throughout my years in the fitness industry, I constantly saw parallels between our spiritual health and our physical health.

When I think of what it means to become a risk taker, I can't help but think of the "progressive training" principle. In simple terms, this means you gain ground in small increments; you make small changes, a step at a time, to give your body the chance to acclimate to the change until it becomes normal and you've established a new threshold. All too often you hear of people who excitedly start exercising and do too much too soon. They injure themselves and end up in worse shape than when they started. Smart athletes, on the other hand, exercise patience and wisdom, focus and forward movement. They take purposeful baby steps toward their goal and keep pushing the limits to move forward. They are intent on gaining ground.

What does this have to do with us? First of all, we are called to be risk takers! Some are more wired for risk taking than others, but we're *all* called to step out of our comfort zone in such a way that if God doesn't come through for us, we'll fall flat on our face. But we take those faith-risks one wise step at a time.

We're not supposed to run haphazardly toward the mission field or to inner-city ministry without training and counsel. Nor are we supposed to shrink back in fear and build a nice comfortable life within our self-defined boundaries. God's charge to us is this: *No shrinking back in fear! No jumping ahead with undeveloped faith! Follow Me and I will take you to places you never imagined.*

We gain ground by taking calculated risks wrapped in wisdom, prayer, and a clear understanding of God's will for us. We say yes to God even if it doesn't fit in with our preconceived ideas for our life. We gain ground by submitting to and learning from seasoned leaders. We grow large in faith by humbly admitting that we appear quite small when we are no longer the queen of our comfort zone.

I love this Gary Haugen quote: "We don't have to try to be brave; we have to train to be brave." *Exactly.* In order to reach the oppressed, the hungry, and the overlooked, we need the courage to go to them. That doesn't mean we all have to go overseas. AIDS hospices exist in practically every city, as do food pantries, nursing homes, soup kitchens, and community outreach centers. Battered women and foster children need a voice and an ally. Refugees who escaped brutal injustice within their home countries need friendship and help as they begin new lives in the United States.

Becoming a risk taker starts with this daring prayer: "Here am I, Lord. Use me. Send me. Lead me out of my comfort zone." That's a risky prayer, and one God is giddy to answer. Remember, He loves us so very much and has so much invested in us that we'll never be out of His care. Embracing God in times of training and refining grants us the treasured privilege of joining Him in His work around the world. His wisdom and timing prepare and protect us. When we put our weight on His promises, we find that He is more than strong enough to hold us.

To become a risk taker is to push—under the Holy Spirit's wisdom and leading—just beyond what's comfortable for us. Yes, our knees will rattle at times. We'll get a bit nauseated after making a commitment that costs us, be it time, money, personal comforts, convenience, and hardest of all—our sense of control. Our mind will tell us all kinds of logical reasons we should not be stepping out in such a way. And we'll be able to come up with lots of good, noble-sounding excuses for staying put!

When Kevin and I sat in the Houston airport waiting to meet up with our IJM team, I noticed a retired couple in their seventies walk into the gate. They were with another church group also headed to Guatemala. I was inspired and challenged by this brave couple. They were up in years and moved slowly through the airport, yet their eyes sparkled with kindness when they met up with the rest of their team. Talk about inspiration!

As long as we have breath, God will have great things for us to do.

Even so, the fears will come. What do we do when we feel in over our head? Read this excerpt from Jim Cymbala's great book, *You Were Made for More*:

> If your faith is weak and you feel overwhelmed by what God is proposing for you to do, spend time in the Bible and at the throne of grace, saying, "Lord, I know I should believe you; I know you keep your promises in your Word. But I'm feeling overwhelmed by what I see. It's too big for me. I can't imagine it happening. Help me, Lord! Give me faith to believe."[2]

Moses took a risk when he faced Pharaoh and demanded he release the slaves. After an intense battle of wills, Moses, under God's direction, led his people out of captivity. Daniel took a risk by standing up for his convictions. As a result, God strengthened him, spared him, and honored him. David took a big giant risk when he faced Goliath. He was outsized, outnumbered, and by far, the youngest one on the battlefield. But God was on David's side and he won. The giant dropped like a sack of potatoes and David threw his arms up in praise.

Ruth took a risk when she left her native land and followed Naomi to a foreign land. That risk and her righteousness landed her in our Savior's lineage. Peter took a risk when he stepped out of the boat to walk with Jesus on the water and had the privilege of participating in a miracle.

Think about Jesus for a moment. He subjected Himself to our human limitations: fatigue, hunger, and temptation. He encountered many wretched things on earth that He never had to deal with in heaven. He came and loved, suffered and endured, all for the sake of love. When I consider that He stepped out of heaven's comforts to rescue me in my poverty and captivity, well, that makes Him all the more heroic to me.

It's in a Christian's spiritual DNA to be a risk taker. Yet we send God a mixed message when we say, "I want all of what You have for me, Lord, but I want to look dignified at all times, keep everyone's respect, and never leave my comfort zone." When we throw self-preservation aside and courageously cry out, "You can have me, Lord!" then we'll see what love can do.

Being a believer involves faith. And faith involves risk—calculated yet heroic steps that lead us out of places of self-protection and into places of God-provision. Embracing our freedom means we are willing to press past our fears because freedom is better. It means we are willing to forgo a few comforts that we may be comforters. It means we are willing to grab hold of God's hand and follow Him to more spacious places, to the edges of our promised land. When God says, "Go!" it's more dangerous to stay behind. There is less risk in moving into the unknown than in lagging behind in disobedience and unbelief.

> Speak up for those who cannot speak for themselves; ensure justice for those being crushed. Yes, speak up for the poor and helpless, and see that they get justice.
> (PROVERBS 31:8-9)

Those who sacrifice essential liberty for temporary safety are not deserving of either liberty or safety.[3]   —Benjamin Franklin

Lord, you have assigned me my portion and my cup; you have made my lot secure. The boundary lines have fallen for me in pleasant places; surely I have a delightful inheritance. I will praise the Lord, who counsels me; even at night my heart instructs me. (Psalm 16:5–7 NIV)

May we never get ahead of God because of our good intentions or blind ambitions. May we never fall behind because of fear or self-ishness. May we stay in step with our wise and wonderful Shepherd who knows us inside and out. And may we stay within the realm of authority and boundaries God set for us, which occasionally will take us beyond our comfort zone and into the faith zone!

 ***Faithful Lord,**

*I want to embrace my freedom! Lead
me out of my comfort zone and into
new places of promise. Awaken my
heart for those I'm appointed to reach and give me a heart
to do Your will. Here am I, Lord, send me. I'm willing to
take risks, to believe Your promises, and to embrace Your
faithfulness. Part the waters, Lord, and lead me to the
next place You have for me.*

*And now, Lord, I pray for the hurting right here in
my community. Help me not to miss them, Lord. Open
my eyes to see where You would be if You lived in my
town. Grant me God-sized faith to take faith-filled
risks when You tell me to. Mobilize the churches in my
community to work together for the sake of the poor, the
hurting, and the lost. Find me faithful, Lord. Amen.*

1. Read Psalm 32:8. Write about an experience when you followed God with absolute clarity from start to finish.
   • Were risks involved? Name them.
   • What's the biggest God-appointed risk you've ever taken? How did it turn out?

2. Read Psalm 32:9. Write about a time when you were hard of hearing.

3. Read Numbers 13:25–30. Notice that taking new and abundant land involves a battle. The majority sees the problem and shrinks back. The risk taker sees the opportunity and presses on. Which are you? Write a prayer asking for more faith.

4. Read Psalm 37:31. What's the best way to stay on the path God has for you? Commit a risk-taking Scripture to memory this week. Press on, my friend!

Shortly after Gladys joined IJM, she was part of a rescue operation to free victims working as forced labor slaves at a brick kiln. She reflects: "All of a sudden we were in a mob, and I didn't think we would come out alive. Later that night I told my children about it. I wasn't sure how they would respond. They asked me why I would risk my life, so I told them. I explained what we are working for, and whom. My older daughter said she wanted to pray for the victims. So now, every time I go on a trip they pray for the people we are going to rescue."

—Gladys, social worker, IJM South Asia

section four

Following
His Lead,
Changing
the World

ALINA'S* STORY

But I trust in your unfailing love. I will rejoice because you have rescued me. —Psalm 13:5

Greatness lies, not in being strong, but in the right use of strength.[1] —Henry Ward Beecher

As a child, Alina* had a difficult home life. One of twelve children living in an impoverished community in the Philippines, she and her family never seemed to have enough to go around.

When a distant aunt asked Alina to stay with her family to care for her child and to assist her around the house, Alina saw a chance for stability. "I instantly said yes," Alina remembers. Alina moved to her aunt's house, eager to leave the chaos of home behind.

In her new home, Alina had food to eat. She had enough money to take the bus to school. She was part of a family.

But everything changed when her aunt's husband returned to the family home. A high-ranking police officer, he had been assigned to a far-off municipality when Alina first moved in.

Upon his return, he sexually assaulted eleven-year-old Alina and threatened her with violence if she told anyone about the abuse.

*Not her real name. Alina's story courtesy © International Justice Mission

Alina had no voice. She was a young girl from a poor family, and her assailant was a man of influence in the community because of his position on the police force. For several months, Alina remained silent—afraid to speak against him or even to tell anyone what had happened. The pain and humiliation of the assault were compounded by the fact that there was no response to it.

"With [my uncle's] return, I faced a prisonlike existence. I was trapped in my brokenness, my silence, and my fears for a long time," Alina recounts.

But someone *was* willing to speak up for Alina. IJM Manila's team of attorneys learned of her case. They worked with local authorities to secure her attacker's arrest and prosecution. Alina now had an advocate for justice.

IJM legal staff is pursuing Alina's case in court. The process has lasted more than five years—in the Philippine judicial system, court proceedings can be particularly protracted—but the trial is moving forward. Alina is not giving up, and neither are the IJM attorneys standing with her.

IJM also filed an official complaint with the Philippine National Police against Alina's uncle, seeking his dismissal from the force. It took more than four years of advocacy on Alina's behalf, but when the Philippine National Police issued their decision, the message was clear: Alina's abuser was dismissed from the force for conduct unbecoming of a police officer.

Today the girl who once had no voice is a young woman of presence with a strong passion for justice. IJM aftercare staff continues to walk alongside Alina as she pursues her goals. She attends college, where she majors in mass communications. "Broadcasting is my passion," she explains. "I want to share with other people the knowledge, the experience, and the lessons that I have learned in life."

Alina also pursues her passion to help others by advocating for and supporting other victims through IJM Manila's Standing To-gether to Advocate Rights (STAR) program. As part of STAR, Alina helps abuse victims to testify against their perpetrators in court—a process that can be extremely difficult. "I can put myself in their shoes and understand them," she says. "I do this to help them come out triumphantly from the situation." Today Alina is a voice of hope to new clients in the Manila office, sharing her story and encouraging them through the process of seeking justice.

For the wicked are moral weaklings but the righteous are God-strong. (Psalm 37:17 MSG)

My friend Susan Ivancie, IJM director of development, donor relations, met Alina while on a trip to the Philippines. Read her story:

When I first met Alina, I thought she was a fellow IJM employee from one of our field offices. She was sharp, articulate, confident, and had a clear understanding of how the aftercare centers work. You can imag-ine my astonishment when I realized this young woman was *once* a vic-tim. I stood there, held her hand, and looked into her eyes. I saw what freedom from fear looked like; I saw courage clearly looking up at me; I saw the face of forgiveness and the choice of love over hate. Best of all, I saw Jesus' unconditional love and grace shining brilliantly at me.

On behalf of every young woman whom evil has tried to poison, I want her (and you) to know that I saw what eternal immunity in Christ looks like. God can and does remove the poison that paralyzes us, and He imparts healing, courage, and wholeness in its place.

If you saw Alina today, you wouldn't recognize her. She isn't fa-mous. While she may seem nondescript by the world's standards, she is profoundly special. Like you, she is a beloved daughter of Christ.

So to my strong sisters who endured and overcame the evil that tried to destroy you, *you* are *not* defined by anyone's action toward you. Ever. You have a depth to your story that is *yours*, as Christ's beloved daughter, to live out to its fullest expression. Never underestimate the full extent of your purpose, passion, and potential. In Christ, you have a beautiful future.

 **Lord,**

I just want to take a moment to thank You for the countless ways You've rescued and redeemed me. If not for You, who knows where I would be? Thank You for putting people in my life to stand up for me, strengthen me, and believe in me. So often I take these things for granted. Thank You, Lord, for never looking away, and for never letting go of me. My hope is in You.

And now, Lord, I pray for sweet, brave Alina. Her courage inspires me to take what the Enemy meant for evil and turn it for the greater good of others. I pray for every young woman who has been victimized in some way. Heal her, restore her, and empower her to make a difference in her world. Don't let the Enemy have the last word! Rise up, O Lord, and make Your presence known in these painful situations. Turn every victim into a victor like Alina! In Your name, I pray. Amen.

No study questions today

19

EMBRACING
THE BIG PICTURE

*Don't shuffle along, eyes to the ground, absorbed with the
things right in front of you. Look up, and be alert to what is
going on around Christ—that's where the action is. See things
from his perspective.* —COLOSSIANS 3:2 MSG

*We are part of the fabric of history. The choices we make, the
things we believe, and the way that we live, directly affect our
society today and our world tomorrow. We as Believers have a
mighty responsibility to embrace our high privilege and to live
in a manner worthy of our calling.*[1] —SUSIE LARSON

One of the many wonderful things we'll enjoy about
heaven will be the ability to listen to the countless stories of how our
lives intersected with others. We'll be amazed to learn how our decisions directly affected their lives on earth. And when we see how
our choices affected the culture around us, I imagine we will, for the
briefest moment, wish we had taken more risks and lived with a bigger perspective.

We need courage to be all and do all that Christ intends for us!
We need faith, tenacity, and a constant reminder to keep the big picture in mind.

The underlying message in this book is about reclaiming lost land, leaving captivity, embracing the suffering, and following God to promised places. How easy—and normal—it is to shrink back when we hear all of the bad news on television, or when a current difficulty rings true to a painful past memory. Since we're relational beings, our insecurities can influence our decision making, which directly affects our tomorrows.

We need to be careful about what we listen to the most, be it negative news or negative repetitive thoughts. We need to pay attention to our tendency to spot an obstacle when God sees an opportunity. Time and again, when we step back and look up, we'll be reminded of the Kingdom call on our life. Even though our days are filled with redundant tasks, we are history makers and world changers. If we forget that very important point, we will live a small and ineffective life.

In fact, my point was just made for me. I was looking for the right word to describe our day-to-day chores. I'm not sure "redundant" is the best choice, but that's the word I punched into my thesaurus. Here's what popped up:

> **Redundant:** *Adjective: many churches are now redundant, unnecessary, not required, inessential, unessential, needless, unneeded, uncalled for; surplus, superfluous.*[2]

The example used above states that many churches are now unnecessary, needless, and superfluous. Of course this definition is written from a secular viewpoint, but it contains some painful truth. Many churches have programmed themselves to death. They experience a form of religion but lack any power, conviction, or passion. They take up space in their community rather than bring life to it. Obviously this is not true of every church; many wonderful churches thrive in our midst. But we have a serious problem in America. Overall the church is on the decline; people are walking away from it totally disillusioned. Someone recently told me that other countries are sending missionaries *to* America because of the poor state of the church here.

Furthermore, much of the church dropped the ball on AIDS, human trafficking, and slavery. We tend to like our Christian bubble and insulate ourselves from the worst parts of society. But Jesus often hung out in the worst parts of town. He touched and blessed the grimy sinner who *knew* she was a grimy sinner. He healed the sick and ate with the outcast. He went to difficult places and left those places better than He found them.

> The righteous care about justice for the poor, but the wicked have no such concern.
>
> (PROVERBS 29:7 NIV)

We must bravely face the world's heartaches and messes because God sees *us* as part of the solution. You know that trouble out there? It's yours. It's mine. I don't mean only human trafficking—which I'm sure you can tell is close to my heart—but this issue reveals the two extremes staring us in the face:

• **Human trafficking.** It's the Devil's desire to destroy young women, to use and abuse girls and women in horrific, evil ways, and to toss them aside like yesterday's trash.

• **Jesus' life, death, and resurrection.** After Jesus rose from the dead, He first appeared to a couple of women. What a picture of God's love for us; He desires to heal, restore, and establish women in Kingdom roles, *making them* joint heirs with Him. He desires to use girls and women in honorable, miraculous, holy, and powerful ways; to set us free and make us whole, and to draw us close to Him as His beautiful bride.

What Jesus offers us has more far-reaching implications than personal freedom. Every choice we make sows a seed upon this earth. We must model Jesus' love—His blessing of freedom—to our daughters and to the young women around us so that the next generation can go where we never dreamed of going.

My friend Susan and I were talking on the phone one day about this very thing. She made an important point when she said, "The Enemy has built a fortress to hold women captive, and every time we stand against injustice, every time we reclaim our God-given land, even if it's only inch by inch, we push against our adversary."

When we through our courage, faith, and conviction stand on the side of justice, we gain momentum for the freedom of those precious souls held captive today and for those who will follow us in history. Like a battering ram, we weaken the Enemy's stranglehold on women.

Righteousness, peace, and joy in the Holy Spirit: that's God's plan. Sin, fear, and oppression: that's the Enemy's plan. Our daily battle is for a greater cause. When we learn holiness at home, we bring holiness into the world. When we die to self when nobody's watching, we bring resurrection life into our encounters with friends and strangers in the world. When we forgive the petty person because we have more important things to do, we make room in our heart to be more compassionate toward those who are *really* suffering.

It matters that we persevere. It matters that we forgive ourselves and accept God's grace to begin again. There's a cloud of witnesses cheering us on, yelling from heaven, "Believe the truth about yourself because it's perfectly wonderful and beautiful! You are loved and called and chosen! Don't live a small life when God has made you for so much more! Believe His promises! Go where He sends you! Trust Him to deliver you. He is faithful and you are loved!"

Does your heart shrink from painful memories or past mistakes? Do you feel as though you're barely hanging on, and you wonder how in the world *you* can make a difference in the world? I'll tell you how: by the power of Christ in you. Even if you are in a fragile season, God is with you there.

> A bruised reed he will not break, and a smoldering wick he will not snuff out, till he leads justice to victory. (Matthew 12:20 NIV)

If we dwell in His presence daily, we can rest with Him there (see Psalm 91:1). He cups His hands around us and protects us from the elements. He breathes life into us. He won't allow us to be snuffed out and He won't allow us to be broken beyond repair. God is on a rescue mission, but He will not walk all over us to achieve His desired end. He wants us with Him. Sometimes *we're* the one who needs rescue and He is always aware of our need. At the right time, He rescues us, restores us, and then sends us out to do the same. He cares for us in the way that He wants us to care for others.

> He would not trample on the dispossessed or underprivileged in order to reach His goals. He would encourage and strengthen the broken-hearted, oppressed person. He would fan even a spark of faith into a flame. His ministry would continue till He would bring justice to victory. His humble, loving care for others would not be extinguished by the hate and ingratitude of men.[3]

His humble loving care for others would not be extinguished by the hate and ingratitude of men. May the fire of our Christlike love and our heavenly perspective burn brightly in the face of hateful, ungrateful people! May we live *in response to God rather than in reaction to others!* That's what it means to embrace the big picture.

Maybe you're not feeling fragile but strong and faith-filled. Use your strength to make a difference in your world. These are important times. The Bible exhorts us to warn the idle, encourage the timid, help the weak, and be patient with everyone (see 1 Thessalonians 5:14).

Let's raise our sword and shield and declare freedom! God is on a rescue mission and He wants us along for the ride. It will cost us to engage in this fight, but oh, the rewards! What spoils we will reap! What victory awaits us! What do you want for your legacy? What are these "last days" going to be about for you?

Life—overflowing with freedom, compassion, courage, and conviction; life marked by faith, hope and love; life surrounded by Spirit-led risks and mighty conquests—that's the life God intends for you and me!

What world-changing objective has God set before you? What will you say to the mountains that stand in your way? Here's what I like to say: "You are bigger than me, but the God in whom I trust is bigger than you! Now be moved into the sea!"

Embrace the bigger picture, dear sister. This is an urgent hour, not a time to bury your head in the sand. History will either bear the burden of your unbelief or the blessing of your obedience.

> But in that coming day no weapon turned against you will succeed. You will silence every voice raised up to accuse you. These benefits are enjoyed by the servants of the Lord; their vindication will come from me. I, the Lord, have spoken. (Isaiah 54:17)

 ***Dear Lord,***

Thank You for being the God of all humanity. We are Yours! Greater are those who are for me than those who are against me. Open my eyes that I may see how great and how mighty You are. Help me to remember that I am never alone. Give me a bigger perspective; help me to discern Your highest and best will in every situation. May I abound in love and wisdom that I may serve You in profound and miraculous ways.

And now, Lord, I come to You today on behalf of my suffering sisters in captivity. The Enemy has gotten away with murder and rape and torture and I say, "No more!" Rise up, O God, and scatter Your enemies! Take this passionate prayer and like a battering ram blow the doors off of the fortress the Enemy has built to oppress women. Go to the darkest places of the earth and shine Your light there. Bring freedom, restoration, and peace. In Jesus' name, I pray. Amen.

1. Read Philippians 1:9–11. I love this passage! Rewrite these verses into a personalized prayer. I did this one month ago and have my prayer memorized. What a power-packed request it is!

2. Read Hebrews 12:1–3 and break up this verse into four parts:
   - **Cloud of witnesses.** How often do you consider the idea that you have a cheering section in heaven? How does that make you feel?
   - **Throw off everything that hinders.** What attitude or belief hinders you from being truly free?
   - **Run with perseverance.** How is your faith-pace right now? Are you running with perseverance? Describe how your race is going.
   - **Fix our eyes on Jesus.** Are you single-minded in your pursuit of Christ right now, or are you distracted? Write down your thoughts.

3. Read 2 Kings 6:14–17. Ponder this passage for a while. Spend some time asking God for His perspective on your life and your world. Write what He tells you.

4. Read 2 Kings 6:15–17. Imagine this scene. Embrace Elisha's faith. Ask for eyes to see. Write a prayer.

5. Read Psalm 34:7. Memorize this verse! And when you're faced with circumstances that threaten your perspective, declare these words out loud: "I have nothing to fear, just more of God to experience!"

"At times, the work we are doing becomes discouraging and it seems that there is no end to the evil that surrounds us. Yet God continually reminds and encourages me that 'the light shines in the darkness, and the darkness has not overcome it' (John 1:5). Wherever the light and truth of Christ are, whether in word or in action, these will transform the darkness."

—LISA, SOCIAL WORKER, IJM CAMBODIA

20

CLAIMING YOUR
GENERATIONAL INFLUENCE

I lavish unfailing love for a thousand generations on those who love me and obey my commands. —EXODUS 20:6

You can be a friend of God and shape history for generations.[1]

—WILLIAM FORD III

In his book *Created for Influence*, William Ford III shares an amazing family story about an heirloom handed down from his forefathers who were slaves on a plantation in Lake Providence, Louisiana. The treasured item is a cast-iron kettle used for cooking (and secretly for prayer).

The slaves were not allowed to pray and endured terrible beatings if they were caught. Can you imagine? So these brave souls used the black kettle for cooking during the day and then sneaked it to the barn at night. They dug a hole in the ground, turned the kettle upside down (propped up by several rocks), got down on their faces, and prayed into the kettle to muffle the sound. They risked their lives to have time with God, but their prayers weren't even for themselves. Regardless of the risk, they pressed heaven for a cause that was beyond them: their children's children's freedom from slavery. They risked their lives for those yet to be born.

Read this excerpt:

One of my ancestors, who was present at these prayer meetings as a young girl, passed down the following information along with the kettle: "These slaves were not praying for their freedom at all. They did not think they would see freedom in their time, so they prayed for the freedom of their children and their children's children. That absolutely amazes me. These friends of God risked their lives to pray for the freedom of their children and the ensuing generations!"[2]

How can we not do the same? While we enjoy literal freedom, our world declines all around us. Oh, that we too would take the risk, inconvenience ourselves, and prayer walk through our cities, interceding for the freedoms of those we may never meet! May we fast and pray for our children that they may stand strong in a crooked and depraved generation. May we send money to those who put themselves in harm's way to free today's slaves. Every dime, every prayer, every time we stand on the side of justice and freedom—because Jesus called us to—we exert our influence over the culture and over future generations.

But what if we do not heed the call? Let's look at this from a different angle. The other night we sat around the dinner table with Troy and Sara Groves and IJM Director of Development Susan Ivancie. We enjoyed a delicious meal and great conversation as we planned our upcoming IJM benefit banquet. We talked about the rise of slavery and how there are more slaves today than there were just ten years ago.

Sara remarked, "I can't help but think how different things would be if we would have been fighting this hard back then. Ten years ago, little boys with broken hearts were sold into slavery or simply left completely abandoned and neglected. Today many of those boys are now angry young men who have joined the militia. We have such a responsibility to stand in the gap, to share God's love, and to let them know that we care. If no one comes for today's children, they will soon be young men and women who are completely lost and filled with hatred and despair."

The ripple effect of our choices is staggering. Not that we can do everything, but we—as *believers* in a most high, miracle-working God—are called to do *some*thing.

Generational ties and influences are strong indeed. Every one of us is influenced by the choices, habits, bondages, or freedoms of our forefathers. Part of embracing our freedom is to identify the unholy bonds that tie us to past generations. Does your background include alcoholism? Gluttony? Materialism? Drug addiction? Depression? Promiscuity? Pessimism? Faithlessness? You must sever the unholy spiritual ties that bind you.

Neil T. Anderson's book *The Bondage Breaker* provides a comprehensive biblical look on how to break free from your past. You can identify some of the generational sins passed down to you even today. Spend time with the Lord praying for clarity on these things. Then

> The curse of the Lord is on the house of the wicked, but He blesses the home of the just.
> (PROVERBS 3:33 NKJV)

when you're ready, ask Jesus to forgive you for strengthening these generational ties (e.g., the choices and sins you've committed consistent with those of your forefathers). Repent of the sins God brings to mind. Intercede for your family by praying, "Forgive us, O Lord, for . . ."

Once you've prayed through your list of generational strongholds, lift your sword (the sword of the Spirit—God's Word—your weapon) and say: "By the power and the authority of Christ in me,

I sever my tie with these generational sins! They will have no part of my life or in the life of my children, or their children's children! We are starting a new heritage, a new generation! One of obedience, faith, and love for the Lord! In Jesus' name I proclaim our freedom from (name them)! *I will* walk in freedom for *I have* sought out the Lord's precepts!"

I will walk about in freedom, for I have sought out your precepts. (Psalm 119:45 NIV)

Don't despair if you repeatedly stumble in those same areas. Simply *bear fruit in keeping with repentance* (Matthew 3:8 ESV) by repenting of your sin, renouncing your connection to the family stronghold, and proclaiming your freedom in Christ. Soon you'll be bearing fruit in the wastelands of your life. Imagine.

Why is this important? Our witness is only as strong as our freedom is real. We can have the most noble convictions in the world, but if we are snarky and impatient when we don't get our way, those things will interfere with our influence. If we gossip more than we pray, those misspoken words will demolish our influence. If our addictions get in the way of living out our convictions, we'll have mostly a negative influence.

Embracing our freedom means being willing to deal relentlessly with the faults and foibles in us that cause others to stumble over us. We don't want one shred of Christ's message of love to get lost in translation through us. If people get irritated with us, may it be because of our unwavering conviction to follow Christ, not because of our constant tendency to be selfish or inconsiderate.

May God increase, and those parts of us decrease! I'm talking to myself here. My selfish love of comfort and protection is strong. I die daily that I might be more useful to Him. When I think of some of the heroic men and women whose humble passions are consumed with loving the least of these, I realize once again that I have such a long way to go. It breaks my heart when I think of how selfish I can be. Yet the Lord still calls us to join Him on His rescue mission. His love and patience with us is quite staggering, wouldn't you say?

> Psychological and sociological studies have confirmed over and over that children who have been abused become abusers. In other words (and this is highly oversimplified), when authority figures are harsh, abusive, evil, and angry they produce harsh, abusive, evil, and angry children and followers. God is not a child abuser. His grace and mercy toward us make us gracious and merciful people. That's why when you encounter Christians who are negative, narrow, and critical, you can rest assured that they haven't been spending much time with God.[3]

This excerpt reminds me of Sara Groves's comment. Children who suffer at the hands of evil people will be deeply affected by their tormentors. These precious children need Christ's influence in their lives, and that's where we come in through our prayers, support, and actions. Furthermore, if we have a past that continues to perpetuate itself in our present circumstances, we too need more of God's influence of freedom in our life. It's *for* freedom that Christ has set us free!

I've met a number of women who were abused as children yet who turned out to be gentle, God-fearing, mighty women of faith. Whatever we've been through in the past, with God's help we can overcome it. The more time we spend in His presence, the more our life will reflect the divine liberty and the enormous influence we have in Christ Jesus.

Embracing our freedom also means being willing to fight for more freedom and influence than our parents enjoyed. May we take what our parents offered us and build on it, push past it, make something more of it, so our children may enjoy a greater level of freedom and influence than we ever did.

As I mentioned earlier in the book, my grandfather was severely beaten over a union dispute in the inner city of Minneapolis when my mom was seven years old. He died later from a brain hemorrhage associated with that beating. I grew up hearing about how scary and dangerous the inner city can be.

While battling my wretched fears, my husband and I have tried to sow seeds of faith and conviction into our kids. The other night my son Jake called me from Nashville and said the greatest thing: "Mom, a bunch of us made some hot meals, gathered some blankets, and went into the inner city to feed, hang out with, and pray for the homeless. It was the best night ever. We met some amazing people."

Praise God. Our fruit is bearing fruit.

The book of Joshua tells us of a prostitute who changed the course of her family's history by one act of faith. Rahab went from living the sordid life of a prostitute to becoming a rescuer of God's people (by hiding the spies from their enemies). She saw the Lord's favor on the Jewish people and took a mighty risk to save them (see Joshua 2).

> Rahab was both clever and wise. She saw judgment coming and was able to devise an escape plan for herself and her family. As soon as she heard what God had done for the Israelites, she cast her lot with his people, risking her life in an act of faith . . . Rahab was like a brand plucked from the fire. Her own people destroyed, she left everything behind, becoming an ancestor of King David and, therefore, one of Jesus' ancestors as well.[4]

Rahab's life is a beautiful illustration for us all. God rescued her from a life of depravity and gave her the opportunity to partner with

Him in an historic way. Isn't it amazing that our filthy ways don't chase God away? He doesn't run *from us*. He sent His Son *to us*, to save us from our destructive tendencies. He intends to make us into something beautiful and brave. I love that about Him.

If there's even a little "yes" in our heart, God moves on it. He helps us get past our weaknesses and frailties and gives us the great privilege and opportunity to influence our culture, which in turn will affect future generations. He loves us. And He loves those who are still lost and still captive. He'll reach them with or without us. May we not pass up this opportunity to be history makers and world changers!

And the Lord said, "Listen to what the unjust judge says. And will not God bring about justice for his chosen ones, who cry out to him day and night? Will he keep putting them off? I tell you, he will see that they get justice, and quickly. However, when the Son of Man comes, will he find faith on the earth?" (Luke 18:6–8 NIV)

Precious Lord,

I want to follow Your lead and change the world. Use me, Lord! Enlarge my faith and my vision for what is possible if I'll only take You at Your Word! These are desperate times calling for mighty faith. May future generations be blessed by the way I live my life. May they enjoy the blessings of my obedience.

And now, Lord, I ask You to break the curse of generational slavery that has its grip on whole communities and family lines. Bring hope to those in captivity. Raise up someone to get the gospel to them that they might be healed and renewed in You. Break the curse of generational slavery and bring freedom to these precious families. In Jesus' name, I pray. Amen.

1. Read Genesis 7:1. Do a little background reading if necessary and answer this question: Why was Noah considered righteous in his generation?

2. Read Deuteronomy 32:20. Spend some time praying, repenting, and interceding for this depraved generation (the influences of media, the squandering of time, the disrespect for authority, the love of money, the disregard for life, and the perversion of sex).

3. Read Judges 2:10 and think about how many Christian families are too busy to stop and share with their children the great things God has done. Make a commitment today to share a few such stories with your children, or with young people who will listen.

4. Read 2 Kings 10:30. What two things did Jehu do to please God? What was the outcome? How do you interpret this passage? What is God asking you to do? Know that God notices and God blesses our efforts to sincerely please Him.

5. Read Psalm 24:3–6. Pray that yours would be a generation to seek God's face!

"You cannot expect people to thank you for what you do to bring justice to them. Ultimately, you can expect to please God. But eventually you hear things like something I heard yesterday: 'Sir, I don't know how to pay you back for what you did for my daughter. I will never forget that . . .' What could I say? Deep in my heart I knew that more than pleasing him, I want to please God."

—PABLO, FIELD OFFICE DIRECTOR, IJM GUATEMALA

EXPERIENCING
RADICAL CHANGE

*Or did you think that because he's such a nice God, he'd let
you off the hook? Better think this one through from the beginning. God is kind, but he's not soft. In kindness he takes us
firmly by the hand and leads us into a radical life-change.*

—ROMANS 2:4 MSG

What God does, he does well.[1]   —JEAN DE LA FONTAINE

It had been a full day of ministry *for Jesus and His disciples. The sun's heat soaked up their stamina as they forged their way through
the crowds. The gentle breeze picked up a layer of dirt from the ground and
dusted the disciples' faces. Dirty and thirsty, the men would have preferred to
steal away hours ago, but Jesus' steadfast purpose kept them going. They
headed for Galilee and took a short cut through Samaria.*

*After walking for hours, the disciples finally reached Samaria. Aware of
their tired bodies and pasty mouths, Jesus sent His disciples to a nearby town
to purchase something for dinner. Meanwhile He sat down by an old well, put
His head back, and rested for a bit.*[2]

While the disciples were away, Jesus had a divine appointment
with a Samaritan woman. Any respectable Jewish man would never
be caught talking with a woman in public, not to mention a Samaritan woman. So for Jesus to talk openly with a Samaritan woman

who was known to be living in sin—well, that broke every religious mold and tradition! But Jesus doesn't stumble over social stigmas when He is on a rescue mission. He crosses every barrier to get to us!

Read the whole story in John chapter 4. Imagine what that moment was like for the Samaritan woman. Sin meets a Savior. Promiscuity meets Purity. Pain and weakness meets Strength and Power. When the Samaritan woman looked into Jesus' eyes, her soul was laid bare. Jesus didn't want what other men wanted from her. He wanted absolute honesty about her predicament and her need. He lovingly yet firmly confronted her sin because He wanted her free. The Samaritan woman had been drinking muddy water from a broken cistern. Jesus stood in front of her and offered her the Living Water for which her soul was made.

We all come to Jesus for salvation by first admitting our need and by confessing our sin. We grow in Him much the same way. Spiritual maturity involves humbling times of refining and fresh awareness of our need for Him. When we humbly come to Jesus, He lifts us to a new realm of understanding.

Jesus offered the Samaritan woman a chance to recognize her need. He confronted her sin. She wasn't quite ready to have the spotlight on her, so she deflected it with excuses and questions.

Being a master communicator, Jesus answered her questions and then brought the conversation back to what *He* wanted to talk about: her captivity. Can you imagine what it was like when that Samaritan woman first realized that freedom and healing were possible for her?

She engaged in a life-changing conversation with her Savior. She found her soul's deepest need met in Him. Excited about this encounter, she left her reason for coming to the well in the first place— her bucket—and returned to the people who had judged her for her promiscuity. This time, instead of running away from people, she ran *to* them.

The Samaritan woman faced the people she had worked so hard to avoid, the ones who gossiped about her promiscuous lifestyle. And in so many words she said to them (at least this is how I picture it), "You know that stuff you've been saying behind my back? Well, first of all, you were mostly right. But come meet a man who said it to my face! Come meet a man who told me everything I've ever done!"

How many jaws dropped to their sandals when they saw this unashamed sinner, who was saved by grace, share her deepest secrets? How can you argue with passion such as that? Freedom on a countenance is hard to miss. When saving grace replaces saving face, everything changes. This woman obviously didn't care what people thought of her anymore. She wanted others to experience the freedom she found in Jesus.

Self-preservation must go if we wish to be and do everything Jesus has in mind for us. Here's another excerpt from my imaginative portrayal of this story:

Two days later is was time for Jesus and His disciples to move on. The townspeople walked their Savior to the edge of town. They extended their arms as the men walked away. They prayed a prayer of blessing on the disciples who left everything to walk with God's Son.

Tears escaped the Samaritan woman's eyes as she watched the men disappear over the hill. She jumped a little when the crowd turned toward her. Holding her breath for a bit, she looked to the side and noticed the dirty pond that had reflected her image just days before. Have they not changed their minds about me as I have thought? *she wondered silently.*

She could not have been more wrong. Within seconds she was enveloped by warm embraces and kind words proclaiming, "Now we believe because we have seen Him ourselves and not just because of what you told us. He indeed is the Savior of the world!"

The Jewish man she had met at the well, this Jesus, did not just improve her. He changed her from the inside out and made her new. Though her eyes could no longer see Him, she would replay His words in her mind forever: "But the water I give, takes away thirst altogether. It becomes a perpetual spring within . . ."

A perpetual spring . . . over and over, again and again, it will never run dry. His love will never dry up, His mercies are new every morning, and His faithfulness extends to every generation.

May your ways be known throughout the earth, your saving power among people everywhere.
(PSALM 67:2)

She would remember this and never thirst again.

I don't have room in this chapter to delve into this story as much as I'd like. But it's one of my favorite speaking messages. The Samaritan woman provides yet another picture of the kinds of people God loves to free, to transform, and to use before a watching world. Imagine how worthless this woman must have felt going from one man to another. But when she met the man Jesus, everything changed. Her life was radically renewed.

Speaking of change, read this wonderful excerpt from IJM President Gary Haugen's November 2008 update letter:

How sweet these words are: *Everything has changed.*

The Rev. Dr. Martin Luther King, Jr. reminded us that "we are called to play the Good Samaritan on life's roadside, but that will be only an initial act. One day we must come to see that the whole Jericho road must be transformed so that men and women will not be constantly beaten and robbed as they make their journey on life's highway." And we have seen that Jericho road change. We see brothels that once sold children shut down. We see scared young girls grow into brave women. We see hope and security replace fear and oppression. We see dignity restored—because you have had the courage to stand with us, as we dream together of justice, of transformed lives, and of renewed hope.[3]

When Jesus steps in, everything changes. Think of those He restored to health, like the lame man at the pool of Bethesda. He was disabled and helpless, yet Jesus put him on his feet again. Consider the woman who bled nonstop for twelve years. Imagine what her life was like: the fatigue, the body odor, the social stigma, the loneliness. In one moment, her life was restored. Her energy returned. She got her life back.

Think of Lazarus. He was dead—and then he lived! What was *that* like? Elizabeth was barren and then conceived a child who became the forerunner of Christ. Consider the disciples. They were once ordinary men, yet through Christ's influence and the Holy Spirit's power they rocked the world in a way that continues even today.

To the extent that we'll allow Jesus to transform our deep, needy places we will partner with Him in transforming others' lives. Jesus is after two specific things in His followers' lives: to heal us and to deal with us. He wants to heal us from our wounds and painful experiences. And He wants to deal with those things in our character that get in the way of our freedom and His message.

In this all-out match against sin, others have suffered far worse than you, to say nothing of what Jesus went through—all that bloodshed! So don't feel sorry for yourselves. Or have you forgotten how good parents treat children, and that God regards you as his children? My dear child, don't shrug off God's discipline, but don't be crushed by it either. It's the child he loves that he disciplines; the child he embraces, he also corrects. God is educating you; that's why you must never drop out. He's treating you as dear children. This trouble you're in isn't punishment; it's training, the normal experience of children. Only irresponsible parents leave children to fend for themselves. Would you prefer an irresponsible God? We respect our own parents for training and not spoiling us, so why not embrace God's training so we can truly live? While we were children, our parents did what seemed best to them. But God is doing what is best for us, training us to live God's holy best. At the time, discipline isn't much fun. It always feels like it's going against the grain. Later, of course, it pays off handsomely, for it's the well-trained who find themselves mature in their relationship with God. (Hebrews 12:4–11 MSG)

Radical change. That's what God is after; that's what people notice. The Samaritan woman had more than words for the townspeople; she had a renewed countenance. Her face was no longer covered with shame. We need more than words for the world around us. We need true freedom, radical change from within that we may become the perpetual spring; the continual source of refreshment Jesus intended us to be.

What kind of *radical* change is God after in your life? Is He asking for more of your time and your trust? Is He putting His finger on an issue that repeatedly presents itself when things don't go your way? Maybe He's confronting your tendency to hide or avoid uncomfortable situations as He did with the Samaritan woman. Or perhaps He is shaking up your personal comforts so that you might remember wherein true security lies.

God is asking *me* for the stretching, reaching kind of faith in every area of my life (physically, financially, emotionally, mentally, and spiritually). And with every inch I stretch with Him, I grow in Him. With every sacrificial cent I give, I become richer. I've never been more stretched than I am right now, but I've never been more alive either. I've never had such a heightened awareness of my sin and selfishness, but I've also never understood God's deep love and high call as I do today.

Jesus always makes things better than they were before. He brings life to dead marriages. He brings healing to sick and injured bodies. He brings restoration to wounded souls. He shines light in dark places. He changes our affections and refines our convictions. He rescues captives and sets us free. And then He makes us stronger than we could ever be on our own. When we walk with Jesus, radical change is good.

As we grow bolder and more tenacious in our freedom, may we be relentless in our efforts to reach out to those who are desperate for radical life change. May our countenance reflect the soul-freedom we enjoy! May the perpetual spring within us be a source of nourishment to those all around us.

Precious Lord,

Change me from the inside out! You desire truth in those inmost places of my being, and in those hidden places, You will make me know wisdom. Help me to spend so much time in Your presence that my countenance glows for all to see. Help me to humbly receive Your correction and discipline because You only discipline those You deeply love. I don't want to play a religious game. I want everything You have for me: full freedom, life abundant, and a deep compassion for others. Change me, Lord!

And now, Lord, I pray for every woman and child stuck in brothels on this earth! Change every brothel into a care center for healing and restoration. Change every hidden den of sin into a house of praise and outreach. Bring change to those who are desperate for rescue. Change the darkness into light, change the slave into a free man, and change the victim into a victor. In Jesus' name, I pray. Amen.

1. Read Matthew 3:8. Are there any ways you are living differently today than you did last year at this time? Has God gotten hold of you in deeper ways since then? Write them down.

2. Read 1 Peter 2:8–9 (the *New Living Translation* if possible). The Rock that strengthens us makes others stumble. Verse 9 states our position in Christ. Write who we are in Him. Write down why God has brought us out of darkness and into the light.

3. Read 1 Peter 2:10. We were once lost but now we're found. Write the two "changes" referred to in this verse. To what extent do these "radical changes" affect your daily life? If your answer is "not too much," then consider why that is. Write down your thoughts.

4. Write a prayer thanking God for such a radical gift.

5. Read John 9:25. Describe an area of your life where "once you were blind but now you see." How did you come upon such a revelation? Write it down. Share your story with someone this week.

"In seeking justice for the women and children trapped in the commercial sex industry, I have learned over and over again the truth of Isaiah 50:10–11. In the dark places, when rescue seems humanly impossible, the answer is always to trust in the name of the Lord and to rely on him. Walking in the light of our own fires and torches leads down a path to torment."

—Patrick, field office director, IJM Cambodia

22

COMMITTING TO FEAR THE LORD

Those who fear the Lord are secure; he will be a refuge for their children. Fear of the Lord is a life-giving fountain; it offers escape from the snares of death.

—PROVERBS 14:26–27

To fear God is to obey Him, even when it does not seem to be to our advantage.[1]

—JOHN BEVERE

One cold Thanksgiving morning several years ago, we took our three teenage sons to the shore of a raging river. We wanted these young men whom we loved so much to have a visual reminder of the important message we were about to convey.

Kevin and I had been distressed by several recent news accounts of Christians who had committed heinous crimes. One particular story hit us between the eyes.

Years ago we were volunteer youth pastors. Weeks before that chilly Thanksgiving morning, we learned that one of our former youth group members had killed his friend's parents. When my husband heard the news, he felt as though someone had slammed him in the chest with two giant fists.

A once nice, polite, clean-cut boy was involved with the murder of two innocent people. We couldn't get our minds around such a tragedy. Kevin was so upset that he couldn't work for the next few hours. Instead, he drove around aimlessly, praying as he tried to grasp how the boy we knew could have committed such a crime. It was horrifying.

Within days of hearing this story, we heard several more stories of Christians who had made unbelievably devastating choices. With a heavy heart and an unsettled spirit, I took my concerns before the Lord. He led me to a passage in Ezekiel 12 where God expressed His anger toward the Israelites for taking His Word lightly. The Israelites had assumed that His prophets' difficult words regarding their sin would amount to nothing. They had lost their fear of the Lord.

I put my Bible on my lap and looked out of the window. I considered how prevalent that same irreverent attitude is in our day. As I bowed my head to pray for my sons and our youth, I sensed God telling me something very profound:

We are in a day of acceleration. Everything is moving faster. The rivers of holiness and evil are raging and each person must choose where he or she wants to go and wants to grow. Where once a bit of anger turned to a brief conflict, it now turns to murder. Where once when people didn't get their way, they got irritated; now they now walk away from God-ordained marriages, churches, jobs, relationships, etc. Take care of your sins while they are still small; otherwise, they will take you where you don't want to go. The river is strong. On the other hand, the river of holiness rages stronger still. For those who esteem My name and walk in My way, they will experience an acceleration in growth, insight, and answers to certain prayers. The Enemy is on the move, but so am I. Walk in the fear of the Lord!

Needless to say, this message from God lit a fire within me! I asked my husband if we could take our sons to a raging river on Thanksgiving morning. And so we did. Bundled in winter garb, with hot coffee and our Bibles, we drove the boys to the spot where the Mississippi and Rum rivers converge. As the five of us stood on the shoreline, we listened to the rushing water and talked about its force. We tossed a few sticks into the river and watched them disappear within seconds.

Each boy sat on a tree stump and cradled his coffee. "What's this about, Mom and Dad?" they asked. Kevin and I knelt in front of our sons and replied, "You've heard the recent news and we've discussed it at length. You know how deeply these events have affected us. We know you are good men and we so appreciate who you are. We also know that it's entirely possible that if you wanted to, you could hide all kinds of things from us. But God sees everything and He's given us a very sobering word.

"Don't take liberties with your freedom. Your faith walk can never be about looking good or saving face, because those efforts will lead you astray. Your walk with the Lord *must* be about humility, righteousness, holiness, faith, hope, and love. Then you have heaven's defenses on your side!

"Guard your hearts in these coming days; don't let the Enemy gain entrance into your life. If you put your toe into the wrong river, it could sweep you off your feet and take you where you don't want to go. We love you so much and see such great potential in each of you. We're asking you to recommit to walking in the fear of the Lord."

After reading a few Scripture passages and talking about the importance of the times, we knelt, confessed our need for more of the Lord in us, and thanked Him for such a sobering message. We each found a stone and wrote on them: The Fear of the Lord—Thanksgiving Day—2005—Ezekiel 12:28.

As I mentioned in chapter 12, a few years ago George Barna released polling data that suggested few differences exist between

American Christians and non-Christians regarding addictions, habits, and the like. At least on paper, it's hard to tell us apart. We may say we believe certain things, but many of us live as *un*believers.

Even in Jesus' day, people disregarded the Lord and ignored the consequences of sin. Matthew 27:35 hits me hard every time I read it: *After they had nailed him to the cross, the soldiers gambled for his clothes by throwing dice.*

In one single verse we read about our Savior's heroic sacrifice *and* man's unbelievable ignorance. The King of the universe hung overhead while the people gambled with their lives below. And so it goes today.

> But as for me, I am filled with power—with the Spirit of the Lord. I am filled with justice and strength.
> (Micah 3:8)

God was active in the world then just as He is today. Though some may deny or ignore His presence, He is still God. Though some may dismiss or disregard His promises, they are still true. *The small remnant,* the few who will walk the narrow path, humbly obey Jesus, and deeply love Him, will get to glimpse heaven on earth. *We* get to participate in the divine nature of the living God. *We* get to walk in His presence as we live here on earth (see Psalm 116:9, my life verse).

The earth responded to Jesus' death on the cross. Rocks split in two and darkness covered the earth. The dead even responded to Jesus' death on the cross. The righteous dead, that is. After Jesus' resurrection, they were raised from the dead, went into town, and appeared to many people. What was that like? And what happened to the unrighteous dead? Well, they stayed dead.

Here's another biblical account of God's power and man's response to it. In Matthew 28 we read of the two Marys who went to the tomb where Jesus was buried. In biblical times women were considered a lesser gender. Since these two women had associated with Jesus, they were especially vulnerable. How brave these Marys were to go to the tomb!

An angel of the Lord appeared before them. His appearance was as lightning and his clothes as white as snow. Imagine the power that surrounded this servant of the Most High God! Once again, the earth responded—it quaked. The big tough guards responded—they became like dead men. And what happened to the two vulnerable Marys?

They were comforted and encouraged. The tough guards slipped into a coma and the vulnerable women were blessed! Imagine! The same sun burns one and warms another.

From an earthly standpoint—at least in America—it's hard to tell many believers from nonbelievers. But heaven clearly knows the difference. Jesus and the angels know who is serious about her faith and who is not. Even the demons know who is a serious contender for freedom and who just talks a good talk.

In these increasingly evil days, many people find God offensive. They don't get the point of obedience or repentance, and call the arrogant blessed. Wicked people put God to the test and seem to get away with it.

> Your words have been hard against me, says the Lord. But you say, "How have we spoken against you?" You have said, "It is vain to serve God. What is the profit of our keeping his charge or of walking as in mourning before the Lord of hosts? And now we call the arrogant blessed. Evildoers not only prosper but they put God to the test and they escape." (Malachi 3:13–15 ESV)

Talk about shaking a fist at God! When we come to such a place of unbelief that we don't think our perspective or our behavior matters, *our* attitudes anger God's heart. When we embrace this mind-set, we wander dangerously close to a raging river of ignorance that threatens to drag us under its current. Though evil seems to prosper at times, God is just. Though the wicked seem to get away with murder, Jesus redeems every situation entrusted to Him. We honor Him because He is God.

As we pursue freedom and fight for others' freedoms, we *will* endure hardships and resistance along the way. We'll be tempted to wonder if God is paying any attention at all.

Will we stand in faith and walk in humility amidst opposition and seeming injustice? Will we revere the Lord and mistrust ourselves enough to keep short accounts with our sin? Will we believe that God is motivated by love, that He is fully aware of the imbalanced scales, and that one day He will set the record straight?

Of course we will stumble or struggle on occasion, but we must never stop honoring God. To fear the Lord means that I will do what He says because I know that He will do what He says. To fear the Lord is to remember who He is. The fear of the Lord is the beginning of wisdom. The more we get to know Him, the more we understand Him (see Proverbs 9:10).

The Lord knows what life on earth is like. He understands the thousands of distractions pointing us away from faith. That's why a faithful, focused heart pleases Him so much.

When amidst our struggles we lift each other up, God takes note. He loves when we cheer each other on and bring perspective to a situation. He's right there in the midst of our desire to live righteously before Him. With every word we speak, with every sacrificial act of love we offer, and with every thought we think that acknowledges God's presence and honors His name—especially in difficult times—heaven observes. God notices our prayers, our thoughts, and our gestures. They are written down, and He holds them close to His heart.

Then those who feared the Lord talked with each other, and the Lord listened and heard. A scroll of remembrance was written in his presence concerning those who feared the Lord and honored his name. "They will be mine," says the Lord Almighty, "in the day when I make up my treasured possession. I will spare them, just as in compassion a man spares his son who serves him. And you will again see the distinction between the righteous and the wicked, between those who serve God and those who do not." (Malachi 3:16–18 NIV)

Heaven clearly distinguishes between those who honor and fear the Lord and those who do not. The day is coming when the earth will see things as heaven does. While we have today, may we be aware of God's presence and power all around us. May we live in a manner worthy of His name. And may we tend to the things God cares about, for that is why we're here.

Precious Lord,

The earth responds to Your presence and so do I! I praise Your beautiful name and thank You for loving me!

Pour out Your Spirit on me in increasing measure. Surround me with Your loving-kindness and compassion that I may have something to impart to others. Heighten my conviction that I may live a life in step with You. It's my greatest honor to be linked in fellowship with You. Lead me on, Lord.

And now, Lord, bring the holy fear of God to the wicked brothel owners and slave traders in our day! Visit them in the night and show them Your mighty power. May their plans fail and their victims be set free! Bless every precious slave and traffic victim with a sense of Your great love. Give them dreams of being free. Write Your Word on their hearts. Give them faith that You're working on their behalf. Set them free and restore them fully! In Jesus' name, I pray. Amen.

initiate your freedom

1. Remember, the same sun that burns up one, heals and restores another. Read Malachi 4:1–3 and notice the contrast between how God's power affects the wicked and the righteous. When you envision that sun of righteousness rising with healing in its wings, what part of you gets healed? Write a prayer thanking God by faith for His divine healing in your life.

2. Read Deuteronomy 29:18–19 and take inventory of your family. Are there family members who seem to think they can go their own way without consequence? Write a prayer for them.

3. Read Deuteronomy 10:12 and break it down.
   - On a scale of 1–10, how aware are you—daily—of God's presence, power, and the consequence of disobedience?
   - How much of your day is spent "walking in His ways"—in other words, living your life as unto Him?
   - Is your love for the Lord increasing or waning? Explain.
   - Are you serving God out of passion and conviction or out of obligation?

4. Read Proverbs 14:27. Explain the truth behind this verse. How has the "fear of the Lord" saved or protected you? Write it down and share your story with someone. This world needs more stories like yours.

"In this age, justice may be a laughable ideal for intellectuals and pragmatists. But for we who are foolish enough to lay down our lives for others as Christ did, it is an attainable reality. Justice is not impossible as long as there are those who feel the pain of the oppressed and are compelled to seek it for them."

—Reynaldo, attorney, IJM Manila

23

DISCOVERING JESUS
IS A GENTLEMAN

*The Lord is my shepherd; I have all that I need. He lets me
rest in green meadows; he leads me beside peaceful streams. He
renews my strength. He guides me along right paths, bringing
honor to his name.* —Psalm 23:1–3

*God is not a supernatural interferer; God is the everlasting por-
tion of his people. When a man born from above begins his
new life, he meets God at every turn, hears him in every sound,
sleeps at his feet, and wakes to find him there.*[1]

—Oswald Chambers

My dad says that I live in the land of the giants. I have to
agree with him. My three sons and my husband all stand over six
feet tall. To most people that isn't huge, but I'm only five foot two,
so the contrast is quite apparent. Sometimes when our family stands
in a circle, the men talk right over my head just to tease me. When
I was first married, one of my biggest adjustments was adapting my
life around my giant husband. He's a big guy and in my little world,
the ground shakes when he moves.

I can't tell you how many times I've been knocked in the nose
just because Kevin moved his arm. One day as we drove to a wed-
ding, Kevin opened our car's center console and reached in to

retrieve a CD. His arm came up so fast that it hit my arm into my face. My cup of soy-chai-latte ended up all over my face, my hair, my purse, and my clothes. I was a gooey mess—and I wasn't too happy about it. Kevin looked at me with eyes wide open and, bless his heart, he didn't know what to say. I looked like someone who had just taken a bath in a vat of nondairy creamer, and we were far away from home. So we pulled into the local Walmart and bought me a new outfit. We laughed about it *later*.

But in all the things that matter, my husband is a gentle giant. He is tender with my fears and insecurities, and he is gentle with me. He simply moves in proportion to his size. One day during my prayer time, I pondered the bigness of God and the vastness of *His* movements. Our Lord put the stars in place. He holds the oceans in His palm. He spoke the world into being; He told the waters where to stop and the land to begin. At the blast of His breath, the bottom of the oceans can be seen. The mountains melt like wax in His presence and all of creation sings His praises. What a mighty God we serve!

How is it that He can move so majestically and yet holds us so close? He is gentle with our fears and insecurities. He comforts us when we are alone. And He promises never to step on us and accidentally take us out of commission. The most powerful force there ever was or ever will be *loves us* and gently moves us through life at a pace we can keep. He divinely restrains His power so that we will not be consumed in His presence. Amazing love.

What's even more astounding is that though God is the source of everything we could ever want or need, He doesn't force Himself on us. Jesus doesn't kick down the door of our heart—not for salvation, not for growth. He knocks and waits. He is a perfect gentleman. But shrinking back, embracing fear more than faith, believing little, and producing sparse fruit are not without consequences. One day our work will be put through the fire and everything done apart from faith and selflessness will burn up.

All of our fake fruit will melt the minute God's blazing judgment touches it. Only what we did out of love for Jesus will last. Only Kingdom work will survive. Some will escape this fiery testing time with their salvation and nothing else. A sobering truth, don't you think? (See 1 Corinthians 3:13–15.)

While we still have today, may we serve Him well. While we still have breath in our lungs and passion in our heart, may we love Him with reckless abandon. May His opinion matter more than others'. While we still have today, may we tend to the things on God's heart.

The world is filled with hungry and homeless people, widows and orphans, slaves and sex-trafficking victims. The world is full of suffering people but Jesus sends us out fully equipped, armed with promises, led by divine intelligence.

This is our chance to please Him with our faith. Not that we're trying to earn His love or merit our salvation; that's impossible. He already died for us and defeated death that we might live and be free. Offering our life as a Kingdom investment is exactly what it sounds like: an offering of love. We can forgo a few comforts and conveniences on earth knowing that He is preparing a beautiful place for us in heaven.

May we never take advantage of His kindness by ignoring His requests! Though He's given us the freedom to squander our time or to invest it, may we choose the latter! Even though He is gentle with our fears and insecurities, may we please Him by our faith and our tenacity!

But seek first his kingdom and his righteousness, and all these things will be given to you as well. (Matthew 6:33 NIV)

Many believers are saved but not free. They are completely wrapped up in their captivity. It doesn't have to be this way. Godliness holds promise for this life and the life to come (see 1 Timothy 4:8). Christ's life in us can revive us *today.*

It stands to reason, doesn't it, that if the alive-and-present God who raised Jesus from the dead moves into your life, he'll do the same thing in you that he did in Jesus, bringing you alive to himself? When God lives and breathes in you (and he does, as surely as he did in Jesus), you are delivered from that dead life. With his Spirit living in you, your body will be as alive as Christ's. (Romans 8:11 MSG)

Imagine if more believers functioned at the high level God intends. Imagine what would happen if the body of Christ rose up and said, "Enough!" to captivity, to poverty, to the Enemy, and to unbelief! Wouldn't it be something if every believer pushed back on the Enemy's attempts to steal from us and keep us in captivity? What if we embraced God's fiery heart for the least of these and refused to be silent for their sake? I do know this: we would change the world.

It's easier to go with the flow than to resist the current of apathy and self-centeredness. But since when has the path of least resistance ever led to any place of significance? Imagine the mark we would make on history if thousands of us stood up for freedom—our soul freedom and the freedom of the millions of slaves alive today. What would happen if we had the courage to stand up, stand in the gap, and gain ground for Christ's sake?

Jesus has given us free will. Will we walk with a spiritual limp? Will we drink muddy water when Living Water has been offered to us? No! The times call for us to spread out our tent curtains to the right and to the left, to make room in our life for God to work, and to operate under an *ever-increasing* sphere of influence. In Him we live and move and have our being (see Isaiah 54:1–5).

Though He is a gentleman who knocks on the door to our heart, Jesus has kicked in one door . . . the one that held us captive! The door swings on broken hinges. Posted on it with a blood-soaked nail is a sign that reads Freedom Granted. Psalm 111:9 reminds us of this powerful truth: *He has paid a full ransom for his people. He has guaran-*

teed his covenant with them forever. What a holy, awe-inspiring name he has!

Jesus paid a staggering price for our salvation and our freedom, and the salvation and freedoms of others. He sets us free that we might become freedom fighters—willing to advocate for those still waiting for release. God loves justice and we will be very near to His heartbeat when we tend to the desires of His heart.

Jesus is a gentleman. He is gentle with imperfect people. He offers new mercies every morning because we need them. He loves us with an everlasting love. Nothing can ever separate us from God's love. We are saved by grace alone.

> For the Lord is righteous, he loves justice; upright men will see his face. (PSALM 11:7 NIV)

Salvation comes to you and me because our sweet Savior said, "I'll go. I'll die for her. I'll give My life in exchange for hers. Take Me instead."

It's hard to imagine such sacrificial love. But by faith, we embrace it just the same. We accept His grace. We count on His mercy. And because of our deep love and gratitude for who Jesus is and what He has done for us, we say yes to His requests and walk forward unafraid.

 **Precious Jesus,**

You are strong beyond measure yet You're gentle with me. How can I ever thank You for Your patience with me? I can't bear to think of who I would be without You. Take me by the hand and lead me to the places You have for me. Fill me with Your courage and Your strength that I may make a difference in this world. I will not wash my hands of the evil in our day. I will not turn my back. And yet I must admit, it's overwhelming to look at it all at once. Help me, Lord, to walk wisely, patiently, and bravely to the places You have for me. No more, no less. I trust You, Lord.

And now, Lord, I pray for my sweet sisters who are in captivity. Set them free that they too might enjoy freedom and an abundant life. Gracious Father, hear my prayers! Confuse and expose their captors' plans. Bless the rescue operations in progress and keep these heroes safe. Cut off the strength of the wicked and increase the power of the godly. This I pray, in Jesus' name. Amen.

initiate your freedom

1. Read Psalm 18:35 from the *English Standard Version*: *You have given me the shield of your salvation, and your right hand supported me, and your gentleness made me great.* Break this verse up into three parts.
   - What do you think it means to have a shield of salvation? Write your thoughts.
   - In general terms, how does God's "right hand" of support show up in your life? Write about a time when you most sensed His strong support. Write a simple prayer thanking Him for His commitment to you.
   - In what ways has the Lord's gentleness made you great? How has His gentleness lifted you up and given you things you don't deserve? Explain.

2. Read Psalm 90:12. Rewrite this verse in your words and list some of your biggest time commitments (asking God for wisdom in making the most of your time).

3. Read John 1:16 and John 8:31. Can you think of an area where you've taken advantage of the Lord's kindness? Has He asked you to do something that you've put off? Have you taken some of His daily gifts for granted? Write a prayer.

4. Read John 8:32. Memorize this verse. Regularly ask the Lord to increase your understanding and discernment of the truth.

5. Read John 8:35–36. Picture yourself as a slave on a plantation. Now picture Jesus coming onto the scene, purchasing your freedom, taking off your shackles, cleaning you up, and giving you fresh clothes to wear. Imagine Him looking into your eyes and saying, "You're a part of My family now. You are no longer captive. You are free. No one can snatch you out of My hand. Trust Me and live free." When you picture this scene, ask yourself if any part of you seems captive still. Spend some time with the Lord, bringing it before Him once again. Write a prayer thanking Him for your freedom even if you don't feel completely free yet.

"The joy of a transformed life outweighs all the grief we may be asked to bear. I find great strength knowing God takes each difficult step with us. He was the first to know our clients' grief, and His heart for justice teaches us to find the least of His brethren, to uphold them and make their pain our own."

—Lawrence, attorney, IJM Manila

24

Seeing Jesus
as the Warrior

Your God is present among you, a strong Warrior there to
save you. —Zephaniah 3:17 msg

Our Lamb has conquered, let us follow him.[1]

—Motto of Moravian Brotherhood

What a journey we've been on! God is on the move for freedom's sake, and we get to join Him on this rescue mission. What an honor it is to serve a living, loving God! With all of my heart I pray that you were inspired, challenged, and provoked to *live up to your great privilege* and *live out your high call.*

Like Corrie ten Boom, may we fight for the freedoms God has promised us! Like Harriet Tubman (and my friends at IJM), may we carry close to our heart the plight of the slave and the suffering. Like Esther, may we stand in the gap for those in need. And like Ruth, may we leave our comfort zone to live consistently in the faith zone. God is searching the world over, looking for those whose hearts are fully devoted to Him. He's searching for faith in the world; may He find it in us!

God has given us some incredible examples of what it means to have heroic compassion and timeless conviction. And now it's our turn. We live in sobering days. Today's world is entrusted to our care. We are God's people and this is our time!

We are on God's mind every moment, on the hour. May we be as aware of Him as He is of us. May God lift us from the lesser affections and obligations that drain our strength and distract us from our call. May God energize us to reach up for that impossible task and reach out to a world in need. God has great things for us to do. May we do them!

> God has redeeming intentions for every area of society, and we as Christians have the privilege of joining Him in that work. . . . We are called to demonstrate the true nature of God and his creation to those around us by faithfully living out the example of Christ, who shared truth, appreciated beauty, insisted on justice, showed compassion, and loved deeply. As we go about our daily lives, may we recognize and manifest the kingdom of God, still coming in all its fullness, yet already here.[2]

In the coming days, following Jesus will become less popular. We'll see many departures from the truth, many "partial gospels" that allow people to manipulate their faith to match their lives. People will become lovers of self and haters of God, betrayers of friends and rejecters of family.

Standing strong in these days isn't for the faint of heart. These times are not for those easily offended or persistently petty. No, such days require deep faith, gritty perseverance, and a conviction to follow Jesus no matter the cost. His loving example paves the way for us that we might continue what He started.

Jesus came to earth as a vulnerable baby. He stepped into His years of ministry with incredible love, humility, authority, compassion, and holiness. He ruled with a strong sense of justice and with wonder-working power. He suffered and died a sinner's death, though He had no shred of guilt in Him. Jesus changed the world, though many disregard Him even today.

We will encounter people who completely miss what we're about. They won't understand why we talk about justice, slavery, and freedom while we live in a free country. They won't understand the opposition we face because they don't swim against the current.

Even so, we keep swimming, forgiving, loving, persevering, and trusting in Jesus. People may miss us, but heaven knows us, and one day we'll stand in glory with our Savior. For now, we redeem the times because of our deep love for the One who redeemed us; we redeem the times no matter what others may think. People may overlook us as they do Jesus, but one day everything will come into plain view.

When Jesus comes again, *all* of earth will know what the demons of hell and the angels of heaven already know: *Jesus Christ is the King of Kings and the Lord of Lords.* He came as an infant but He's coming back as a warrior. He's coming to claim His reward. And we are that reward. Lord, make us ready.

Then I saw heaven opened, and a white horse was standing there. Its rider was named Faithful and True, for he judges fairly and wages a righteous war. His eyes were like flames of fire, and on his head were many crowns. A name was written on him that no one understood except himself. He wore a robe dipped in blood, and his title was the Word of God. The armies of heaven, dressed in the finest of pure white linen, followed him on white horses. From his mouth came a sharp sword to strike down the nations. He will rule them with an iron rod. He will release the fierce wrath of God, the Almighty, like juice flowing from a winepress. On his robe at his thigh was written this title: King of all kings and Lord of all lords. (Revelations 19:11–16)

I pray that we can raise our expectations of what is possible when we walk with God! And may we lower our expectation that this journey be comfortable or that things should always go our way. Amidst this fight of faith, our weaknesses will be exposed—*but His grace is sufficient.* Our fears will come to the surface—*but His perfect love will cast out every fear.* We'll feel very human at times—*but heaven will never see us that way because Jesus is alive and well in us!*

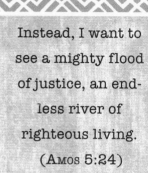

Instead, I want to see a mighty flood of justice, an endless river of righteous living.
(Amos 5:24)

God does not want us to live in fear, hoard what we have, or hide who we are. It's time to step up and step out. The earth is full of God's presence and promises! *God is striding ahead of you. He's right there with you. He won't let you down; he won't leave you. Don't be intimidated. Don't worry* (Deuteronomy 31:8 MSG).

Just how will you change history? What impossible task has God assigned to you? Will you dare to ask Him? The world needs your influence! You may have a thousand reasons for avoiding this Kingdom call, and you may feel far from qualified. Thankfully, that's beside the point. Jesus carefully guards His treasure in you. He is preparing you. He's *been* preparing you! You are ready *today* to step out in certain ways. And your call for tomorrow is greater still. Boldly declare, "Here I am, Lord! Send me!" Don't let your doubts override your destiny. You are called to something more.

Read this excerpt from Jim Cymbala's wonderful book, *You Were Made for More*:

If God's Spirit is upon you, no résumé is too weak. If God is calling you to something more, your perceived lack of qualifications is no longer relevant. God's strength is far greater than your weakness. God's grace is much stronger than your fears. And His plan is not subject to your objections.[3]

You've been so wonderful to pray for the slaves and the oppressed regularly. I pray that you'll continue to remember those who are still captive and for the brave souls trying to rescue them.

I'd like to close with a Franciscan blessing and a love letter from the Lord. Be blessed and enjoy:

May God bless you with discomfort at easy answers, half-truths, and superficial relationships, so that you may live deep within your heart.

May God bless you with anger at injustice, oppression, and exploitation of people, so that you may work for justice, freedom, and peace.

May God bless you with enough foolishness to believe you can make a difference in this world, so that you can do what others claim cannot be done.

And the blessing of God, who Creates, Redeems, and Sanctifies, be upon you and all you love and pray for this day, and forevermore. Amen.[4]

—Franciscan Blessing

 ***My Beloved One,***

I am here with you, every step of the way. I will not desert you. No! I will strengthen and uphold you with My righteous right hand. Reach up for all that seems out of your reach. I will make up the difference. I'm giving you a new walk and a new talk. I'm taking you to places you never imagined. Only trust Me now, or you'll never get there. My highest and best plans for you require love, courage, and faith, and I am the Source of all of these. You will trample down your fears, doubts, anxieties, and insecurities and you'll be strengthened as you go. Have I not said that I bless the diligent and reward those who earnestly seek after Me? You are Mine and I am yours. My banner over you is love. Take this journey one step at a time. Stay focused, stay purposeful and believe Me for great things. You've delighted in Me all these years and now it's My great delight to establish you. Wrap your arms around Me and hang on. We've got a ride ahead! I love you so much and I am right here beside you.

    Your beloved Redeemer

Thank you for going on this journey with me.
My prayers are with you and I too am cheering you on!
Peace and freedom to you and yours.
Susie Larson

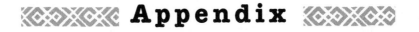# Appendix

GETTING INVOLVED

I hope that as you've learned of our loving Father's heart for justice, you've yearned to participate in this work. Here are some action steps from International Justice Mission to help you become more involved in answering this vital call. More information on any of these steps is also available at IJM's website, www.IJM.org.

- *Pray.* The work of prayer for victims of injustice is urgent—and I hope it will not cease after you have completed this devotional journey. Visit International Justice Mission's website to sign up as a Prayer Partner. You'll receive a weekly e-mail update detailing the urgent needs of IJM staff and those they serve. You can also learn about opportunities to attend IJM's annual Global Prayer Gathering—a powerful time of fellowship and prayer with its staff from around the world.

- *Learn.* Take some time to educate yourself about the justice issues our brothers and sisters around the world face. IJM's website is a great starting point for this. There you will find resources about IJM's work to combat modern-day slavery, sex trafficking, illegal land seizure, sexual violence, and other forms of abuse.

- *Mobilize.* Bring your community with you in this journey. Share with others what you've learned. Attend an IJM benefit dinner together (visit IJM's website to see if one is scheduled in your area). Study God's heart for justice in your small groups.

Commit with another sister in Christ to pray regularly for victims of oppression. Talk about what you've learned with your church leadership and invite your pastor to explore IJM's ministry resources on its website.

- *Give.* Become a Freedom Partner with International Justice Mission. Make a monthly commitment to pay for the rescue the poor cannot afford. So many around the world are waiting for rescue—and are desperate to know they're not alone. How glorious it is to participate in answering their prayers through a financial commitment to justice!

- *Lead.* Bring your family into the work of justice with you. Share with your children what you've learned and connect them with IJM's student ministries. The IJM website can equip your children to hold a Loose Change to Loosen Chains fundraising drive at their school or church. College students can also learn how to bring the message of justice and raise a voice of advocacy in their community by starting or joining an IJM campus chapter.

- *Advocate.* Raise your voice in support of antislavery policies through IJM's Justice Campaigns. You'll find resources to share about your concern for the oppressed with your government representatives on the Justice Campaigns section of IJM's website. Together we can bring a voice for the global poor to the halls of power—and support policies that can bring help to victims of violent oppression.

- *Incorporate.* Add justice to the good works of mercy and compassion you may already be engaging in. IJM's website has resources for short-term mission teams to help you develop the eyes to see and the ears to hear injustice as you travel abroad.

NOTES

Let's Start Here . . .

1. H. A. Ironside, Quotemeal from Heartlight (www.heartlight.org).
2. Gary Haugen, *Just Courage* (Downers Grove, IL: InterVarsity Press, 2008), 64.

Section One: Facing Evil, Recovering What's Ours
Sandana's* Story *(used with permission of IJM)*

1. Adapted from Gary Haugen's book *Just Courage* (Downers Grove, IL: Inter-Varsity Press, 2008).
2. Abraham Lincoln, Quotemeal from Heartlight (www.heartlight.org).
3. Info from IJM's "Forced Labor Slavery Fact Sheet" (www.ijm.org).

Chapter 1: Recovering Lost Territory

1. Quote from prayer flip calendar, "Waiting on the Lord: 101 Thoughts of Hope and Encouragement" (Fort Worth, TX: Brownlow), Thought #58.

Chapter 2: Embodying Truth and Courage

1. Joseph Joubart, Quotemeal from Heartlight (www.heartlight.org).
2. My contemporary retelling of Esther and Mordecai's messages. The last paragraph of the dialogue was taken from Esther 4:13–14 MSG.
3. Ann Spangler and Jean E. Syswerda, *Women of the Bible* (Grand Rapids, MI: Zondervan, 1999), 259–260.

Chapter 3: Transcending Evil and Pain

1. C. S. Lewis, Quotemeal from Heartlight (www.heartlight.org).
2. Thomas à Kempis, Quotemeal from Heartlight (www.heartlight.org).
3. Jennifer Kennedy Dean, *Secrets Jesus Shared* (Birmingham, AL: New Hope Publishers, 2007), 37–38.
4. Kay Warren, *Dangerous Surrender* (Grand Rapids, MI: Zondervan, 2007), 103.

Chapter 4: Putting Fear in Its Place

1. Helen Keller, Questionspage.com, *The Door*, 1957.

2. Kay Warren, *Dangerous Surrender* (Grand Rapids, MI: Zondervan, 2007), Francis Fénelon quote referenced on 32–33.

3. Gary Haugen, *Just Courage* (Downers Grove, IL: InterVarsity Press, 2008), 108.

4. Henry Blackaby, Quotemeal from Heartlight (www.heartlight.org).

Chapter 5: Standing Fast for Freedom

1. Martin Luther King Jr., Quotemeal from Heartlight (www.heartlight.org).

2. "Resolute," *Oxford American Writer's Thesaurus*, compiled by Christine A. Lindberg (Oxford Universty Press, 2004), s.v. "resolute."

3. Ace Collins, *Stories Behind Women of Extraordinary Faith* (Grand Rapids, MI: Zondervan, 2008), 64.

4. Background information on Harriet Tubman from *Stories Behind Women of Extraordinary Faith*, 67–68 and "America's Story from America's Library," (www.americaslibrary.gov).

5. Collins, *Stories Behind Women of Extraordinary Faith*, Harriet Tubman quote referenced on 68–69.

6. Ibid., Jim Cymbala, *You Were Made for More*, (Grand Rapids, MI: Zondervan, 2008), 16.

Chapter 6: Reclaiming Your Identity

1. Meister Eckhart, Quotemeal from Heartlight (www.heartlight.org).

2. Susie Larson, *The Uncommon Woman* (Chicago, IL: Moody, 2008), 26.

Section Two: Believing God Is True to His Word
Maite's* Story *(used with permission of IJM)*

1. Seneca, Quotemeal from Heartlight (www.heartlight.org).

Chapter 7: Embracing Others' Sufferings

1. Sara Groves, personal conversation with author.

2. Andrew Murray, *Believing Prayer* (Minneapolis, MN: Bethany House, 1980, 2004), 85.

3. *Draper's Book of Quotations for the Christian World* (Wheaton, IL: Tyndale, 1992), Billy Graham quote referenced on 495.

4. Murray, *Believing Prayer*, 29.

5. William MacDonald, *Believer's Bible Commentary* (Nashville, TN: Thomas Nelson, 1989, 1990, 1992, 1995), 984.

Chapter 8: Waiting for God to Act

1. Bob Sorge, *Secrets of the Secret Place* (Lee's Summit, MO: Oasis House, 2001), 130–131.

Chapter 9: Rejecting Captivity's Comforts

1. Jonathan Edwards, Quotemeal from Heartlight (www.heartlight.org).

2. William MacDonald, *Believer's Bible Commentary* (Nashville, TN: Thomas Nelson, 1989, 1990, 1992, 1995), 73.

Chapter 10: Finding Refuge in God's Promises

1. Mary W. Tileston, *Joy & Strength* (New York: Barnes & Noble, 1993), George Body quote referenced on 274.

2. "Jesus, What a Wonder You Are" by Dave Bolton.

3. Susie Larson, *Alone in Marriage* (Chicago, IL: Moody, 2007), 165–166.

4. Corrie ten Boom, *Clippings from My Notebook* (Nashville, TN: Thomas Nelson: 1982), 41–42, story referenced in "Psalm 91: God's Shield of Protection" (2005), 119.

Chapter 11: Disarming the Past

1. Mary W. Tileston, *Joy & Strength* (New York: Barnes & Noble, 1993), Horace Bushnell quote rferenced on page 205.

2. "Mien's Story," IJM Update, December 3, 2008.

3. "Disarm," *Oxford American Writer's Thesaurus*, compiled by Christine A. Lindberg (Oxford Universty Press, 2004), s.v. "disarm."

Chapter 12: Refusing to Blend In

1. *Draper's Book of Quotations for the Christian World* (Wheaton, IL: Tyndale, 1992), Oswald Chambers quote referenced on 8086.

2. Ibid., Warren Wiersbe quote referenced on 4125.

3. William Penn, Quotemeal from Heartlight (www.heartlight.org).

4. William MacDonald, *Believer's Bible Commentary* (Nashville, TN: Thomas Nelson, 1989, 1990, 1992, 1995), 57.

5. A. W. Tozer, *The Pursuit of God* (Camp Hill, PA: Christian Publications, Inc., 1995), 149.

Section Three: Trusting God to Be Big in Us

Claire's* Story *(used with permission of IJM)*

1. *Draper's Book of Quotations for the Christian World* (Wheaton, IL: Tyndale, 1992), John Bunyan quote referenced on 5024.

Chapter 13: Taking Every Thought Captive

1. *Draper's Book of Quotations for the Christian World* (Wheaton, IL: Tyndale, 1992), Oswald Chambers quote referenced on 7752.

2. Courtney Helgoe, "See It, Believe It," *Experience Life* magazine (January/February 2006).

Chapter 14: Allowing God to Reduce Us

1. William MacDonald, *Believer's Bible Commentary*, (Nashville, TN: Thomas Nelson, 1989, 1990, 1992, 1995), 2203.

2. Information taken from Roberts Liardon, *God's Generals* (New Kensington, PA: Whitaker House, 2008), 392.

3. Ibid., 393.

4. MacDonald, *Believer's Bible Commentary*, 2204, J. H. Jowett quote referenced in "Life in the Heights," 247–48.

5. Bruce Wilkinson, *Secrets of the Vine* (Sisters, OR: Multnomah, 2001), 75.

Chapter 15: Honoring God

1. *Draper's Book of Quotations for the Christian World* (Wheaton, IL: Tyndale, 1992), Richard Owen Roberts quote referenced on 4650.

Chapter 16: Embracing God's Heart for Justice

1. Gary Haugen, *Just Courage* (Downers Grover, IL: InterVarsity Press, 2008), 65.

2. *New Spirit-Filled Life Bible* (Nashville, TN: Thomas Nelson, 2002), quote from "Kingdom Dynamics Study Notes," 840.

3. Haugen, *Just Courage*, 79–80.

Chapter 17: Taking New Land

1. Jim Cymbala, *You Were Made for More* (Grand Rapids, MI: Zondervan, 2008), 15–16.

2. G. K. Chesteron, Quotemeal from Heartlight (www.heartlight.org).

3. Author unknown, Quotemeal from Heartlight (www.heartlight.org).

Chapter 18: Becoming a Risk Taker

1. *Draper's Book of Quotations for the Christian World* (Wheaton, IL: Tyndale, 1992), Cliff Richards quote referenced on 11487.

2. Jim Cymbala, *You Were Made for More* (Grand Rapids, MI: Zondervan, 2008), 176.

3. Toby Mac and Michael Tate, *Under God* (Bloomington, MN: Bethany House, 2004), Benjamin Franklin quote referenced on 153.

Section Four: Following His Lead, Changing the World

Alina's* Story *(used with permission of IJM)*

1. *Draper's Book of Quotations for the Christian World* (Wheaton, IL: Tyndale, 1992), Henry Ward Beecher quote referenced on 5284.

Chapter 19: Embracing the Big Picture

1. My quote.

2. "Redundant," *Oxford American Writer's Thesaurus,* compiled by Christine A. Lindberg (Oxford Universty Press, 2004), s.v. "redundant."

3. William MacDonald, *Believer's Bible Commentary* (Nashville, TN: Thomas Nelson, 1989, 1990, 1992, 1995), 1249.

Chapter 20: Claiming Your Generational Influence

1. William Ford III, *Created for Influence* (Grand Rapids, MI: Chosen Books, 2007), 72.

2. Ibid., 73–74.

3. Steve Brown, *Approaching God* (Nashville, TN: Random House, 1996), 121.

4. Ann Spangler and Jean E. Syswerda, *Women of the Bible* (Grand Rapids, MI: Zondervan, 1999), 100, 102.

Chapter 21: Experiencing Radical Change

1. *Drapers Book of Quotations for the Christian World* (Wheaton, IL: Tyndale, 1992), Jean De La Fontaine quote referenced on 4993.

2. My imaginative portrayal of Jesus with His disciples.

3. Gary Haugen, IJM Update Letter, November 2008.

Chapter 22: Committing to Fear the Lord

1. John Bevere, *The Fear of the Lord* (Lake Mary, FL: Charisma House, 1997, 2006), 183.

Chapter 23: Discovering Jesus Is a Gentleman

1. *Drapers Book of Quotations for the Christian World* (Wheaton, IL: Tyndale, 1992), Oswald Chambers quote referenced on 4829.

Chapter 24: Seeing Jesus as the Warrior

1. Motto of Moravian Brotherhood, Quotemeal from Heartlight (www.heartlight. org).

2. Quote from daily planner, "YWAM Personal Prayer Diary" (Seattle, WA: YWAM Publishing, 2009), 28–29.

3. Jim Cymbala, *You Were Made for More* (Grand Rapids, MI: Zondervan, 2008), 174.

4. Franciscan Blessing, author unknown.

Appendix: Getting Involved

By Lori Poer, IJM Writer and Media Specialist.

ACKNOWLEDGMENTS

No other book has been as much a labor of love for me as this one. From the start, its topic seemed too big, too out of my reach. But God loves it when we join Him in seemingly impossible tasks. And He gives us everything we need to accomplish His purposes. One of the provisions I love most is the gift of community. Please indulge me as I thank the many people who contributed to this project.

Thank you to Lori Poer, IJM Writer and Media Specialist, for your support, your kindness, and your help with all things IJM. Bless you for making the time for me!

To our IJM benefit cochairs, Troy and Sara Groves: We are so very blessed and honored to serve with you. Thank you for being such shining examples of what it means to be the hands and feet of Christ. And thanks to Susan Ivancie, IJM Director of Development, for your strong support and friendship.

To Connie Padmore, IJM Director of Development, Special Events, and to the whole IJM benefit banquet team: You've become family and we praise God for you! Here's to many more years of standing together for the sake of justice!

To my very dear friends at Moody Publishers: You are the best publisher a girl could ask for. A special thanks goes to Paul Santhouse for your incredible commitment to this project. Thanks to my publicist and my friend, Janis Backing. You always go the extra mile—and I always notice. Bless you. And thank you to my editor, Jane Johnson Struck. You stepped into the task of editing this book with finesse and grace, and you brought clarity to my message. I so enjoyed working with you!

I'm also thankful for the best literary agent in the world. Thank you, Beth Jusino, for knowing me so well and for representing me with such integrity. You are a true gift from the Lord.

To my group of sample readers affectionately known as my Freedom Fighters: Susan Stuart, Patty Fischer, Bonnie Newberg, Janet Nelson, Judy Chesla, Kay Blake, Andie Munn, Carolyn Crust, Daryl Jackson, Lisa Larson, Patty Larson, Barbie Odom, and a special thanks to Lynn Ferguson. Thank you for walking with me through each chapter. Bless you for your brutal honesty and for your constant encouragement.

A special thank-you to Carrie Kuiken for helping me get organized. Bless you for all of your hard work! Thank you, too, to Clay Fandre and to Wendy's parents for allowing me to tell my friend Wendy's story.

I don't know what I'd do without my team of intercessors. Bless you, dear friends, for covering me when I travel, when I'm home writing, and when I'm facing the giants in my path. May God redeem every minute you've spent on your knees for me! I love and appreciate you all.

To my parents, Pat and Ed Erickson: Thank you for sacrificing so much for your kids. I love you to pieces.

To my husband, Kevin: I keep wondering where God is going to lead us next. You're the one I want to serve alongside. I love you. And to my beautiful sons, Jake, Luke, and Jordan: Now that you're grown and have a faith of your own, may you continue to follow Jesus to radical places, may you give of yourselves sacrificially, and may you live with abounding faith. You are priceless to me.

And finally, to Jesus: Thank You for setting this captive free. No matter where I go or what I do, I'll always know and remember who I was before You rescued me. You are a mighty warrior and a perfect friend. I'll follow You forever.

Final Note:
The author is donating 50 percent of her royalties to International Justice Mission to secure justice for those still waiting for rescue.

ABOUT THE AUTHOR

With enthusiasm, humor, and conviction, author/speaker Susie Larson has spoken to thousands of women locally, nationally, and internationally. She is a member of the Advanced Writers and Speakers Association, Women in Christian Media, and served on the board of directors for the Christian Authors Network. Susie also serves an occasional guest host for *Along the Way*—a two-hour talk radio show (AM Faith 900).

Susie's books include *Balance That Works When Life Doesn't* (Harvest House–05), *Alone in Marriage* (Moody–07), *The Uncommon Woman* (Moody–08), and *Growing Grateful Kids* (Moody–10). Susie works as a freelance writer for Focus on the Family, and has been featured as a guest on radio and TV programs across the country, including Moody's *Midday Connection, Family Life Today, Chris Fabry Live!, The Harvest Show,* and the *LIFE Today Show* with James and Betty Robison.

While in Washington D.C., Susie and her husband, Kevin, along with national recording artist Sara Groves and her husband, Troy, represented International Justice Mission's concerns in meetings with Congress as part of their efforts to abolish human trafficking and slavery. The four of them serve as co-chairs for the IJM benefit banquet in Minnesota. Susie comes with a passion to share the love of a Savior who will never let go of us.